PERFORMANCE RESULTS
OF MULTINATIONALITY

PERFORMANCE RESULTS OF MULTINATIONALITY

Ahmed Riahi-Belkaoui

QUORUM BOOKS
Westport, Connecticut • London

Library of Congress Cataloging-in-Publication Data

Riahi-Belkaoui, Ahmed, 1943–
    Performance results of multinationality / Ahmed Riahi-Belkaoui.
      p. cm.
    Includes bibliographical references and index.
    ISBN 1–56720–277–2 (alk. paper)
    1. International business enterprises—United States—Finance.
    2. Investments, American.   3. Stock price forecasting—United
    States.   4. Productivity (Economic theory)   I. Title.
    HG4027.5.R5   1999
    658.15'99—dc21   98–44554

British Library Cataloguing in Publication Data is available.

Library of Congress Catalog Card Number: 98–44554
ISBN: 1–56720–277–2

First published in 1999

Quorum Books, 88 Post Road West, Westport, CT 06881
An imprint of Greenwood Publishing Group, Inc.
www.quorumbooks.com

Printed in the United States of America

The paper used in this book complies with the
Permanent Paper Standard issued by the National
Information Standards Organization (Z39.48-1984).

10 9 8 7 6 5 4 3 2 1

To my family, here and there

Contents

Exhibits

Preface

Multinationality, or the degree of internationalization reflected in the activities of firms, is a key factor of the global economy. Firms view the expansion of their foreign activities as a necessary strategy of survival and performance. In recent years, questions have arisen about the performance results of a multinationality strategy and the adequacy of such multinational strategy. Accordingly, this book presents the results that support the crucial role of multinationality in the financial performance of firms.

Chapter 1 verifies the three features of the eclectic paradigm (ownership advantages, locational advantages, and internalization advantages) as well as behavioral and financing considerations. The evidence and recommendations validate this restatement of the eclectic paradigm of international production by showing that multinationality is positively related to the investment opportunity set, the level of foreign assets, the difference between the rate of return on foreign assets and total assets, the corporate reputation deflated by size, and leverage.

In Chapter 2, we examine the value-relevance of multinational firms by examining the association between the market value of equity and three different measures of multinationality based on accounting data mandated by SFAS No. 14. The three measures are foreign earnings, foreign assets, and foreign revenues. The measures of multinationality and domesticity are found to have significant positive associations with the market value of equity. The evidence and recommendations are that the association coefficient of domesticity is significantly larger than the association coefficient of multinationality, especially for firms with a high level of corporate reputation. Multinationality as measured by earnings provided the largest association with market value followed by revenues and assets.

Chapter 3 uses the Ohlson-Feltham valuation model to examine the relationship between the market value of a firm's stock and the book value of equity. The hypothesis of a positive relationship between multinationality and the market value of the firm is confirmed, adding credence to the "hidden asset" view of multinationality.

The value-relevance of earnings, cash flows, multinationality, and corporate reputation is examined in Chapter 4. The significant results of the impact of earnings, cash flows, multinationality, and corporate reputation provide standard setters with important evidence supporting the additional disclosure of relevant nonaccounting information such as the level of multinationality and the state of corporate reputation.

As Chapter 5 confirms, the market reacts more favorably the larger (smaller) the cash flows (accruals), and the preference of cash flows over accruals will arise under conditions of high multinationality and high reputation.

In Chapter 6, we examine the relationship between the level of multinationality and managers' accounting choices. It is argued that the level of multinationality affects net income and net worth and thereby political costs and political risk. This relationship provides management an incentive to reduce political costs and political risk associated with using income-decreasing accruals. The evidence and recommendations indicate that managers of firms with a high level of multinationality make accounting choices to reduce reported earnings.

Chapter 7 analyzes the association between multinationality and systematic risk as measured by the market model beta. Unlike previous studies, this study suggests that the systematic risk is positively related to the level of multinationality after controlling for corporate reputation and other factors known to be associated with systematic risk. The difference in results is due to a consideration of growth opportunities as measured by the investment opportunity set. While systematic risk is negatively related to multinationality for high investment opportunity set firms, it is positively related to multinationality for low investment opportunity firms.

We examine the role of multinationality and profitability as determinants of the investment opportunity set in Chapter 8. The results confirm a significant positive relationship with multinationality and profitability conditioned by inflation, growth rate, size of the firm, and the index of business formation. The results point to the salient role of multinationality and profitability in creating growth opportunities for the firm.

Chapter 9 considers whether the investment opportunity set of a firm is associated with corporate financing, and whether such association varies over firms with different levels of multinationality. The findings support the contingency view of the relationship between the investment opportunity set and corporate financing. They show a link between capital structure, the investment opportunity set, and multinationality. At different multinationality levels, different investment opportunity sets influence capital structure strategies.

Chapter 10 focuses on whether disclosure policy, level of economic risk, and the nature of the alignment of financial and tax accounting explain differences in financial analysts' forecast error internationally. The evidence is that the level of the error is negatively related to the level of disclosure requirements of global stock exchanges, and positively related to the levels of economic risk and alignment of financial and tax accounting.

Finally, Chapter 11 presents a model of the determinants of the investment opportunity set of multinational firms. Using a sample of U.S. multinational firms, the evidence validates the model by showing growth opportunities, as measured by the investment opportunity set, to be positively related to corporate reputation, multinationality, size, and profitability, and negatively related to leverage and systematic risk.

This book will be of interest to executives in multinational firms, researchers in international accounting and finance, and students in all areas of international business.

Many people helped in the development of this book. I received considerable assistance from the University of Illinois at Chicago research assistant Belia Ortega. I would also like to thank Eric Valentine and Betty Pessagno at Greenwood Publishing for their continuous and intelligent support. Finally, to Janice and Hedi, thanks for making everything possible and enjoyable.

1

Empirical Validation of a General Model of International Production

INTRODUCTION

The eclectic paradigm of international production by multinational enterprises (MNEs) argues that the initial act of foreign production by enterprises and the growth of such production depend crucially on the configuration of three elements: firm-specific (or ownership-specific) advantages, country-specific (or locational) advantages, and internalization advantages.[1-3] While, as argued by Dunning,[4] it remains a robust general framework for explaining and analyzing not only the economic rationale of economic production but many organizational and impact issues in relation to MNE activity, it can also accommodate extensions to allow for firm-specific behavioral differences and financing differences.[5] This chapter first restates such a general model of international production combining both the three features of the eclectic paradigm and the behavioral and financing differences in an operationally testable manner. Second, empirical evidence is provided to validate this restatement and possible extensions of the eclectic paradigm of international production.

A GENERAL MODEL OF INTERNATIONAL PRODUCTION

The general and operationally testable paradigm of international production rests on a combination of the three tenets of the eclectic paradigm and behavioral and financing considerations. As shown in Exhibit 1.1, the model argues that the growth in international production as measured by the level of multinationality is a function of:

a. The ownership advantages as measured by the investment opportunity set of the MNEs

b. The locational advantages as measured by the level of the MNEs' foreign assets

c. The internalization advantages as measured by the difference between the rate of return in foreign assets and the total rate of return of the MNEs

d. The behavioral considerations as measured by an index of corporate reputation deflated by a measure of size

e. The financing considerations as measured by a leverage ratio

The rationale for the model and the choice of measures follows.

Ownership Advantages

The eclectic paradigm of international production specifies ownership advantages as one of the three determinants of the extent, form, and pattern of international production. They include both proprietary know-how (unique assets) and transactional advantages that outweigh the costs of servicing an unfamiliar or distant environment. Basically, the firm has unique ownership advantages that its competitors do not have. These unique ownership advantages are the future investment options of the firm. The firm may be viewed as a combination of assets-in-place and future investment options. The lower the proposition of firm value represented by assets-in-place, the higher the growth opportunities. Myers[6] describes these potential investment opportunities as call options whose values depend on the likelihood that management will exercise them. Like call options, the growth options represent real value to the firm. These growth options are intangible assets or ownership advantages that represent the investment opportunity set.

The multinational firm is a collection of valuable options and generates

Exhibit 1.1
General Model of International Production

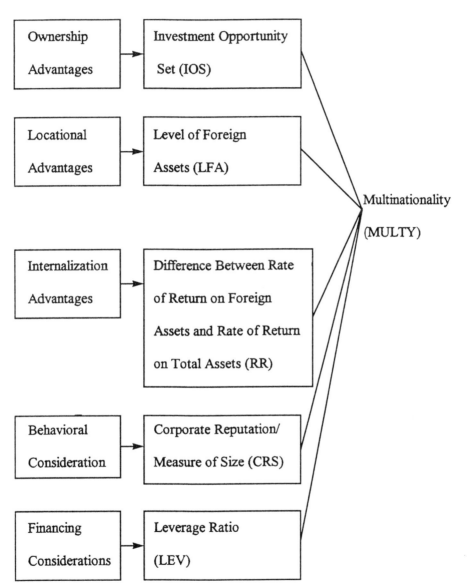

profits that enhance its value.[7] The arbitrage benefits result from (a) the exploitation of various institutional imperfections; (b) timing options; (c) technology options; and (d) staging options.[8,9] Better financing bargains[10] as well as capital availability[11] are also possible through internationalization. In addition, multinational firms can achieve arbitrage benefits in financing cash flows by (a) exploiting financial bargains; (b) reducing taxes on financial flows; and (c) mitigating risks or shifting them to agents with a comparative advantage in bearing them.[12]

This definition of multinationality as a collection of options and arbitrage benefits suggests a positive relationship with growth options as defined by the investment opportunity set. Following the first tenet of the eclectic paradigm, the level of multinationality will be a function of the level of investment opportunity set.

Locational Advantages

The eclectic paradigm of international production specifies locational advantages as the second determinant of the extent, form, and pattern of international production. Basically, the benefits of MNEs are associated with locating certain activities in particular countries. When it is to the best interest of the MNEs to locate their activities in other than the home country, the MNEs are using their locational advantages to respond to a kind of spatial market failure, basically "internalizing exogenous spatial imperfections."[13] The size of the investment located in particular countries indicates the extent and the saliency of the locational advantages.

Following the second tenet of the eclectic paradigm, the level of multinationality of an MNE will be a function of the level of foreign assets as a surrogate measure of locational advantages.

Internalization Advantages

The internalization advantages are the third level of the eclectic paradigm of international production. They refer to the relative benefits associated with serving foreign markets. With internalization advantages present, it is to the benefit of the MNEs to transfer their ownership advantages abroad rather than sell them. The perceived great costs of transactional failure lead the MNE to transfer its advantages across national borders rather than by contractual agreements with foreign firms. As argued by Rugman,[14] the MNE has in a sense "internalized" the market for its use. The MNE will proceed with the internalization if the rate of return on foreign assets is superior or equal to the rate of return on total assets.

Following the third tenet of the eclectic paradigm, the level of multinationality of an MNE will be a function of the difference between the rate of return on foreign assets and the rate of return on total assets.

Firm-Specific Behavioral Differences

One extension of the eclectic paradigm of international production is the consideration of firm-specific behavioral differences.[15] Basically, MNEs adopt specific strategies to define their international posture. While these strategies may not be known to the general public, they are reflected in the reputation of the firm.

The reputation of a firm is important for various decisions ranging from resource allocation and career decisions to product choices, to name only a few.[16] It is an important signal of the firm's organizational effectiveness. Favorable reputations can create favorable situations for firms that include: (1) the generation of excess returns by inhibiting the mobility of rivals in an industry[17]; (2) the capability of charging premium prices to consumers[18]; and (3) the creation of a better image in the capital markets and to investors.[19] To create the right impression or reputation, firms signal their key characteristics to constituents to maximize their social status.[20] In fact, corporate audiences were found to construct reputations on the basis of accounting and market information or signals regarding firm performance.[21-23] These reputations have become established and constitute signals that may affect the actions of firms' stakeholders, including their shareholders. Specifically, a good reputation can be construed as a competitive advantage within an industry.[24] This implies that investors incorporate reputation in determining firm value. Firms with good reputation are more prone to engaging in international production. *Therefore, the level of multinationality will be a function of the firm's reputation.*

Financing Advantages

Another extension of the eclectic paradigm of international production is the consideration of firm-financing differences.[25] It arises from Aliber's[26] dissatisfaction with the eclectic paradigm and his focus on financing as a determinant of multinationality. The MNE uses different currencies to acquire foreign assets, taking advantages of structural or transactional imperfections in international capital and foreign exchange markets. It is the ability to finance investments in different currencies that characterizes the uniqueness of the MNE. This ability to finance part of its production in its home currency and other parts in other currencies depends on the ability of the firm to raise capital, that is, on its leverage. *Therefore, the level of multinationality will depend on the financial leverage of the MNE.*

RESEARCH MODEL

In this study, a regression of the level of multinationality of U.S. MNEs against the variables of investment opportunity set, foreign assets, leverage, differences in ratios of return of foreign assets and total assets, and corporate reputation is presented as evidence of the validity of a restatement and possible extensions of the eclectic paradigm of international production. The model is expressed as follows:

$$MULTY_{jt} = \alpha_{0t} + \alpha_{1t}IOS_{jt} + \alpha_{2t}LFA_{jt} + \alpha_{3t}RR_{jt} + \alpha_{4t}CRS_{jt} + \alpha_{5t}LEV_{jt} + E_{jt}$$

where:

$MULTY_{jt}$ = Level of multinationality for firm j in year t.

IOS_{jt} = Investment opportunity set for firm j in year t.

LFA_{jt} = Logarithm of foreign assets for firm j in year t.

RR_{jt} = Difference between the rate of return in foreign assets and the total rate of return for firm j in year t.

CRS_{jt} = Corporate reputation delated by a measure of size for firm j in year t. Measures of firm size to be used include (a) total assets, (b) total revenues, (c) total cash flow, and (d) number of employees.

LEV_{jt} = Leverage ratio equal to buy long debt/total assets for firm j in year t.

Data and Sample Selection

The population consists of firms included in *Forbes'* Most International 100 American manufacturing and service firms and *Fortune'*s surveys of corporate reputation from 1987 to 1993. The security data are collected from the CRSP return files. The accounting variables are collected from COMPUSTAT. The derivations of multinationality, corporate reputation, and investment opportunity set variables are explained later. The final sample includes 323 firm-year observations that have all the variables over the period of analysis.

Measuring Multinationality

Previous research has attempted to measure the following attributes of multinationality:

1. *Performance*—in terms of what goes on overseas[27]
2. *Structure*—in terms of resources used overseas[28]
3. *Attitude or Conduct*—in terms of what is top management's orientation[29]

Sullivan[30] developed nine measures of which five were shown to have a high reliability in the construction of a homogeneous measure of nationality: (1) foreign sales as a percentage of total sales (FSTS), (2) foreign assets over total assets (FATA), (3) overseas subsidiaries as a percentage of total subsidiaries (OSTS), (4) top management's international experience (TMIE), and (5) psychic dispersion of international operations (PDIO).

In this study we follow a similar approach by measuring multinationality through three measures: (1) foreign sales/total sales (FSTS), (2) foreign profits/total profits (FPTP), and (3) foreign assets/total assets (FATA).

Descriptive statistics and correlations among the three multinationality measures are shown in Exhibit 1.2. Correlations among the variables are positive, and with one exception, all are significant. The nonsignificant correlation is between FPTP and FATA. The low correlations between FPTP, FSTS, and FATA indicate that each variable can make a unique contribution as a multinationality measure. Thus, a factor analysis of all observations is used to isolate the factor common to the three measures. Exhibit 1.3 reports the results. One common factor appears in the intercorrelations among the three variables, as the first eigenvalue alone exceeds the sum of the commonalities. The common factor is significantly positively correlated with the three measures. These factors scores were used to measure the degree of multinationality of firms in the sample.

Exhibit 1.2

Descriptive Statistics and Correlations of Three Measures of Multinationality for *Forbes'* The Most International 100 U.S. Firms

Panel A: Descriptive Statistics

	FP/TP[a]	FS/TS[b]	FA/TA[c]
Maximum	914.3	93	91
Third Quartile	61.9	47.4	41.4
Median	41.3	36.7	30.5
First Quartile	25	25.7	22.6
Minimum	0.2	6.6	2.7
Mean	52.81	37.45	39.92

Panel B: Correlations

	FT/TP	FS/TS	FA/TA
FP/TP	1.000		
FS/TS	0.280	1.000	
FA/TA	0.034	0.193*	1.000

*Denotes p-value < 0.05.
[a]FP/TP = Foreign profits/total profits
[b]FS/TS = Foreign sales/total sales
[c]FA/TA = Foreign assets/total assets

Measuring Corporate Reputation

The independent variable of reputation is the combined score obtained in an annual *Fortune* magazine survey. This survey covers every industry group comprising four or more companies. The industry groups are based on categories established by the U.S. Office of Management and Budget (OMB). The survey asks executives, directors, and analysts in particular to rate a company on the following eight key attributes of reputation:

1. Quality of management
2. Quality of products/service offered
3. Innovativeness
4. Value as long-term investment
5. Soundness of financial position

Exhibit 1.3
Selected Statistics Related to a Common Factor Analysis of Three Measures of Multinationality for *Forbes'* The Most International 100 U.S. Firms

1. Eigenvalues of the Correlation Matrix:

Eigenvalues	1	2	3
	1.3615	0.9680	0.6705

2. Factor Pattern

FACTOR 1

	FS/TS	FP/TP	FA/TA
	0.80529	0.50172	0.67918

3. Final Communality Estimates: Total = 1.361489

	FS/TS	FP/TP	FA/TA
	0.648491	0.251718	0.461280

4. Standardized Scoring Coefficients

FACTOR 2

	FS/TS	FP/TP	FA/TA
	0.59148	0.36850	0.49885

5. Descriptive Statistics of the Common Factor Extracted from the Three Measures of Multinationality

Maximum	2039.24
Third Quartile	74.70
Median	57.03
First Quartile	40.76
Minimum	5.17
Mean	64.35

6. Ability to attract/develop/keep talented people
7. Responsibility to the community/environment
8. Wise use of corporate assets.

Ratings were on a scale of 0 (poor) to 10 (excellent). The score met the multiple-consistency ecological model view of organization effectiveness. For the purpose of our study, the 1987 to 1993 *Fortune* magazine surveys were used. The use of the overall score rather than factor analysis of the eight scores is based on the facts that: (a) it is the overall score that is published in *Fortune* magazine rather than the eight scores on the attribute, and (b) it is then the overall score that is perceived by the readers as well as the respondents of the survey as the reputation index. From previous experience, the respondents know that the means of their scores on the eight attributes will be published as the overall score of reputation. For the purpose of this study the overall score of reputation is deflated by a measure size.

Measuring the Investment Opportunity Set

Because the investment opportunity set is not observable there has not been a consensus on an appropriate proxy variable. Similar to Smith and Watts[31] and Gaver and Gaver[32] we use an ensemble of variables to measure the investment opportunity set. The three measures of the investment opportunity set used are market-to-book assets (MASS), market-to-book equity (MQV), and the earnings/price ratio (EP). These variables are defined as follows:

MASS = [Assets − total common equity + shares outstanding* share closing price]/Assets

MQV = [Shares outstanding* share closing price]/total common equity

EP = [Primary EPS before extraordinary items]/share closing price

Descriptive statistics and correlations among the three measures of the investment opportunity set are shown in Exhibit 1.4. Correlations among the three variables are significant. The low correlations indicate that each variable makes a unique contribution as measure of the investment opportunity set. The results of the factor analysis are shown in Exhibit 1.5. One common factor appears to explain the intercorrelations among the

Exhibit 1.4
Descriptive Statistics and Correlations of Three Measures of the
Investment Opportunity Set for *Forbes'* **The Most International 100 U.S.**
Firms

Panel A: Descriptive Statistics

	MASS[a]	MQV[b]	EP[c]
Maximum	6.4943	60	0.5175
Third Quartile	1.8556	3.1851	0.1081
Median	1.2905	1.9090	0.0713
First Quartile	1.0618	1.2666	0.0482
Minimum	0.8745	4.3333	2.1536
Mean	0.3081	2.7020	0.0638

Panel B: Correlation

	MASS	MQV	EP
MASS	1.000		
MQV	0.0399*	1.000	
EP	0.0158*	0.0230*	1.000

*Denotes p-value < 0.05.
[a]MASS = Market-to-book assets
[b]MQV = Market-to-book equity
[c]EP = Earnings/price ratio

three individual measures. It is used here as a measure of the investment opportunity set.

RESULTS

Panel A of Exhibit 1.6 reports descriptive statistics used in our tests and panel B shows correlations among the variables. These correlations show that all the correlations between MULTY and the other variables in the study are significant at the 0.01 level. The significant associations among some of the variables indicate some degree of collinearity among the independent variables in the regression analysis. However, the max-

Exhibit 1.5
Selected Statistics Related to a Common Factor Analysis of Three Measures of the Investment Opportunity Set for *Forbes'* The Most International 100 U.S. Firms

1. Eigenvalues of the Correlation Matrix: Total = 3 Average = 1

Eigenvalue	1	2	3
	1.0540	0.9868	0.9592

2. Factor Pattern

   FACTOR1

	MASS	MQV	EP
	0.62821	0.66411	0.46722

3. Final Communality Estimates: Total = 1.053994

	MASS	MQV	EP
	0.394651	0.441045	0.218299

4. Standardized Scoring Coefficients

   FACTOR1

	MASS	MQV	EP
	0.59603	0.63009	0.44329

5. Descriptive Statistics of the Common Factor Extracted from the Three Measures of the Investment Opportunity

Maximun	9.3595
Third Quartile	3.2200
Median	2.0450
First Quartile	1.5085
Minimum	2.5209
Mean	1.9812

Exhibit 1.6
Descriptive Statistics and Correlations

Panel A: Descriptive Statistics[a]

Variables	Mean	Standard Deviation	Minimum	25%	Median	Maximum
MULTY	54.723	33.132	6.2109	37.3224	51.1514	418.685
IOS	52305	120138	16.5372	5289.2	13614	1048948
LFA	12.655	1.0913	10.7142	11.869	12.4091	16.1078
RR	0.0062	0.1887	-3.6832	-0.0087	0.0069	0.2894
CRS	0.0008	0.00066	0.00002	0.00022	0.00070	0.00287
LEV	1.109	5.7555	0.3588	0.0275	0.0655	57.8261

Panel B: Correlations [b]

	MULTY	IOS	LFA	RR	CRS	LEV
MULTY	.					
IOS	0.2363*	.				
LFA	0.1407*	0.4417*	.			
RR	-0.3558*	0.1082*	0.0478	.		
CRS	0.1106*	-0.3058*	-0.7677*	-0.3437	.	
LEV	0.0996*	-0.0701	-0.0068	0.00152	0.0844	

[a]Total observations: 323 firm-year observations.
[b]Pearson correlations are below the diagonal.
*Significant at $\alpha = 0.01$.

imum condition index in all regression is only 4.43. As suggested by Belsley et al.,[33] mild collinearity is diagnosed for maximum condition indices between 5 and 10 and severe collinearity over 30. Thus, collinearity does not seem to influence our results.

For each of the multivariate regressions to be reported, we performed additional specification tests, including checks for normality and consideration of various scatter plots. A null hypothesis of normality could not be rejected at the 0.01 level in all cases, and the plots revealed some heteroscedasticity but no other obvious problems. Therefore, we calcu-

Exhibit 1.7
Regression Results of Linear Models

	Model 1 [2]	Model 2	Model 3	Model 4
Intercept [1]	-203.732	-31.566	-41.102	-74.297
	(-12.688)*	(-2.476)*	(-3.298)*	(-5.482)*
IOS	0.000014	0.000032	0.000029	0.000034
	(2.248)*	(3.829)*	(3.659)*	(4.297)*
LFA	17.882	5.653	6.449	8.5599
	(15.284)*	(5.752)*	(6.676)*	(8.446)*
RR	176.953	167.977	161.859	165.100
	(9.961)	(7.532)*	(7.495)*	(7.891)*
CRS	27936	5804.73	421.601	1600.68
	(15.027)*	(5.168)*	(7.084)*	(8.583)*
LEV	0.3113	0.7989	0.8798	0.6384
	(2.693)*	(2.672)*	(3.054)*	(2.268)*
Adjusted R^2	0.5676	0.3179	0.3614	0.3997

[1]*Variable Definitions*
IOS = Investment opportunity set
LFA = Logarithm of foreign assets
RR   = Difference between the rates of return in foreign assets and total assets
CRS = Corporate reputation deflated by size
LEV = Leverage ratio
[2]*Model Differences*
The number differ in the measure of size used to deflate corporate reputation. Size
is measured by total assets in Model 1, cash flow in Model 2, profit in Model 3, and
number of employees in Model 4.
*Significant at $\alpha = 0.01$.

lated the t-statistics after correcting for heteroscedasticity in the manner
described by White.[34]

Exhibit 1.7 presents the results of four regressions that differ in the
way corporate reputation was deflated. Size is measured by total assets
in Model 1, cash flow in Model 2, net profit in Model 3, and rank of
employees in Model 4. In all four cases multinationality was found to
be positively related to the investment opportunity set, the logarithm of
foreign assets, the difference between the rates of return of foreign assets
and total assets, corporate reputation, and leverage. R^2 was the greatest
(56.76 percent) when corporate reputation was deflected by total assets.

The results verified the restatement and possible extensions of the eclectic paradigm of international productions.

CONCLUSIONS

A general model of international production that combines the three tenets of the eclectic paradigm and behavioral and financing considerations is tested using a sample of U.S. MNEs. The evidence validates this restatement and possible extensions of the eclectic paradigm of international production by showing that multinationality is positively related to the investment opportunity set, the level of foreign assets, the difference between the rates of return on foreign and total assets, the corporate reputation deflated by size, and leverage. The results are dependent on the choice of surrogate measures used for the measurement of ownership advantages, locational advantages, internalization advantages, and behavioral and financing considerations. Future research is needed to examine the sensitivity of the results to other potential surrogate measures.

NOTES

1. John H. Dunning, *Explaining International Production* (London: Unwin Hyman, 1988).

2. John H. Dunning, "The Eclectic Paradigm of International Production: A Restatement and Some Possible Extensions," *Journal of International Business Studies* 19, no. 1 (1986): 1–32.

3. Alan M. Rugman and Alain Verbeke, "A Note on the Transnational Solution and the Transaction Cost," *Journal of International Business Studies* 23, no. 4, (1992): 761–771.

4. Dunning, *Explaining International Production*, 1.

5. Ibid.

6. S. Myers, "Determinants of Corporate Borrowing," *Journal of Financial Economics* 5 (1977): 147–75.

7. George Tsetsekos, "Multinationality and Common Stock Offering," *Journal of International Financial Management and Accounting* 3 (1991): 1–16.

8. John H. Dunning, "Reappraising the Eclectic Paradigm in an Age of Alliance Capitalism," *Journal of International Business Studies* 26 (1995): 461–492.

9. Bruce Kogut, "Foreign Direct Investment as a Sequential Process," in C. P. Kindelberger and D. B. Audretsch, eds., *The Multinational Corporation in the 1980s* (Cambridge, MA: MIT Press, 1983): 38–56.

10. F. Giavazzi and A. Giovannini, *Limiting Exchange Rate Flexibility: The European Monetary System* (Cambridge, MA: MIT Press, 1989).

11. D. Eiteman and A. Stonehill, *Multinational Business Finance* (Boston: Addison-Wesley, 1986).

12. Tsetsekos, "Multinationality and Common Stock Offering," 1–16.

13. A. M. Rugman, *Inside the Multinationals: The Economics of International Markets* (New York: Columbia University Press, 1981).

14. Ibid.

15. Dunning, *Explaining International Production.*

16. G. R. Dowling, "Managing Your Corporate Images," *Industrial Marketing Management* 15 (1986): 109–115.

17. R. E. Caves and M. E. Porter, "From Entry Barrier to Nobility Barriers," *Quarterly Journal of Economics* 91 (1977): 421–434.

18. B. Klein and K. Leffler, "The Role of Market Forces in Assuring Contractual Performance," *Journal of Political Economy* 85 (1981): 615–641.

19. R. P. Beatty and J. R. Ritter, "Investment Banking, Reputation, and Underpricing of Initial Public Offerings," *Journal of Financial Economics* 15 (1986) 213–232.

20. A. M. Spence, *Market Signaling: Information Transfer in Hiring and Related Screening Process* (Cambridge, MA: Harvard University Press, 1974).

21. C. Fombrum and M. Shanley, "What's in a Name? Reputational Building and Corporate Strategy," *Academy of Management Journal* 33 (1990): 233–258.

22. Ahmed Belkaoui, "Organizational Effectiveness, Social Performance and Economic Performance," *Research in Corporate Social Performance and Policy* 12 (1992): 143–155.

23. Ahmed Riahi-Belkaoui and E. Pavlik, "Asset Management Performance and Reputation Building for Large U.S. Firms," *British Journal of Management* 2 (1991): 231–238.

24. Fombrum and Shanley, "What's in a Name?," 233–258.

25. Dunning, *Explaining International Production.*

26. R. Aliber, "Money, Multinationals and Sovereigns," in C. P. Kindelberger and D. B. Audretsch, *The Multinational Corporation in the 1980s* (Cambridge, MA: MIT Press, 1983).

27. Dunning, "Reappraising the Eclectic Paradigm," 461–492.

28. John M. Stopford and Louis T. Wells, *Managing the Multinational Enterprise* (New York: Basic Books, 1972).

29. Howard V. Perlmutter, "The Tortuous Evaluation of the Multinational Corporation," *Columbia Journal of World Business* 4 (January-February 1969): 9–18.

30. D. Sullivan, "Measuring the Degree of Internationalization of a Firm," *Journal of International Business Studies* 25 (1994): 325–342.

31. C. W. Smith and R. L. Watts, "The Investment Opportunity Set and Cor-

porate Financing, Dividend and Compensation Policies," *Journal of Financial Economics* 32 (1992): 263–292.

32. J. J. Gaver and K. M. Gaver, "Additional Evidence on the Association between the Investment Opportunity Set and Corporate Financing, Dividend, and Compensation Policies," *Journal of Accounting and Economics* 16 (1993): 125–160.

33. D. Belsley, E. Kuh, and R. Welsch, *Regression Diagnostics: Identifying Influential Data and Source of Collinearity* (New York: Wiley, 1980).

34. H. A. White, "Heteroskedasticity-Consistent Covariance Matrix Estimator and a Direct Test for Heteroskedasticity," *Econometrika* 10 (1980): 817–838.

SELECTED READINGS

Aliber, R. "Money, Multinationals and Sovereigns." In C. P. Kindelberger and D. B. Audresch, *The Multinational Corporation in the 1980s.* Cambridge, MA: MIT Press, 1983.

Beatty, R. P., and J. R. Ritter. "Investment Banking, Reputation, and Underpricing of Initial Public Offerings." *Journal of Financial Economics* 15 (1986): 213–232.

Belkaoui, Ahmed. "Organizational Effectiveness, Social Performance and Economic Performance." *Research in Corporate Social Performance and Policy* 12 (1992): 143–155.

Belsley, D., E. Kuh, and R. Welsch. *Regression Diagnostics: Identifying Influential Data and Source of Collinearity.* New York: Wiley, 1980.

Caves, R. E., and M. E. Porter. "From Entry Barrier to Nobility Barriers." *Quarterly Journal of Economics* 91 (1977): 421–434.

Dowling, G. R. "Managing Your Corporate Images." *Industrial Marketing Management* 15 (1986): 109–115.

Dunning, John H. "The Eclectic Paradigm of International Production: A Restatement and Some Possible Extensions." *Journal of International Business Studies* 19, no. 1 (1988): 1–32.

———. *Explaining International Production.* London: Unwin Hyman, 1988.

———. "Reappraising the Eclectic Paradigm in an Age of Alliance Capitalism." *Journal of International Business Studies* 26 (1995): 461–492.

Eiteman, D., and A. Stonehill. *Multinational Business Finance.* Boston: Addison-Wesley, 1986.

Fombrum, C., and M. Shanley. "What's in a Name? Reputational Building and Corporate Strategy." *Academy of Management Journal* 33 (1990): 233–258.

Gaver, J. J., and K. M. Gaver. "Additional Evidence on the Association between the Investment Opportunity Set and Corporate Financing, Dividend, and

Compensation Policies." *Journal of Accounting and Economics* 16 (1993): 125–160.

Giavazzi, F., and A. Giovannini. *Limiting Exchange Rate Flexibility: The European Monetary System.* Cambridge, MA: MIT Press, 1989.

Hartman, H. H. *Modern Factor Analysis*, 3d ed. Chicago: University of Chicago Press, 1976.

Klein, B., and K. Leffler. "The Role of Market Forces in Assuring Contractual Performance." *Journal of Political Economy* 85 (1981): 615–641.

Kogut, Bruce. "Foreign Direct Investment as a Sequential Process." In C. P. Kindelberger and D. B. Audretsch, eds. *The Multinational Corporation in the 1980s.* Cambridge, MA: MIT Press, 1983: 38–56.

Myers, S. "Determinants of Corporate Borrowing." *Journal of Financial Economics* 5 (1977): 147–175.

Perlmutter, Howard V. "The Tortuous Evaluation of the Multinational Corporation." *Columbia Journal of World Business* 4 (January-February 1969): 9–18.

Riahi-Belkaoui, Ahmed, and E. Pavlik. "Asset Management Performance and Reputation Building for Large U.S. Firms." *British Journal of Management* 2 (1991): 231–238.

Rugman, A. M. *Inside the Multinationals: The Economics of International Markets.* New York: Columbia University Press, 1981.

Rugman, Alan M. and Alain Verbeke. "A Note on the Transnational Solution and the Transaction Cost." *Journal of International Business Studies* 23, no. 4 (1992): 761–771.

Smith, C. W., and R. L. Watts. "The Investment Opportunity Set and Corporate Financing, Dividend and Compensation Policies." *Journal of Financial Economics* 32 (1992): 263–292.

Spence, A. M. *Market Signaling: Information Transfer in Hiring and Related Screening Process.* Cambridge, MA: Harvard University Press, 1974.

Stopford, John M., and Louis T. Wells. *Managing the Multinational Enterprise.* New York: Basic Books, 1972.

Sullivan, D. "Measuring the Degree of Internationalization of a Firm." *Journal of International Business Studies* 25 (1994): 325–342.

Tsetsekos, George. "Multinationality and Common Stock Offering." *Journal of International Financial Management and Accounting* 3 (1991): 1–16.

White, H. A. "Heteroskedasticity-Consistent Covariance Matrix Estimator and a Direct Test for Heteroskedasticity." *Econometrika* 10 (1980): 817–838.

2

The Valuation of the Multinationality of U.S. Multinational Firms

INTRODUCTION

The globalization of the economy and the rapid integration of capital markets have mainly resulted in an expansion of the foreign operations, or multinationality, of U.S. firms in the last twenty-nine years. As a result, the *Statement of Financial Accounting Standards No. 14: Financial Reporting for Segments of a Business Enterprise*[1] (henceforth SFAS No. 14) mandated specific disclosure requirements. These include the disclosure of foreign earnings, foreign assets, and foreign revenues that can be used to provide accounting-based measures of multinationality.[2]

Using data on the breakdown of earnings, assets, and revenues with domestic and foreign components, the study considers three questions: (1) Are the levels in domestic and foreign components of earnings, assets, or revenues associated with the level of the market value of the firm? (2) which foreign component provides the highest association? and (3) are the domestic and foreign components of earnings, assets, or revenues capitalized by the market at the same rate? For a sample of 418 firm-year observations over fiscal years 1986 to 1990, the study finds measures of both multinationality and domesticity have significant positive association with the market value. In the three cases examined, the association coefficient of domesticity is significantly larger than the association coefficient of multinationality. Multinationality as measured by income provided the largest association with market value followed by revenues and assets.

Prior research on the market value-relevance of the disclosure of foreign financial data on a firm's foreign operations relied on return/changes regressions for estimating the price earnings regression and did not evaluate the impact of different accounting-based measures of multinationality.[3-8] This study differs in two counts. First, it uses price level regression rather than return/changes regression based on the argument that in situations where prices lead earnings, price level regressions are better specified. Second, it focuses on three SFAS No. 14 mandated data that can be used for the measurement of multinationality: foreign earnings, foreign assets, and foreign revenues.

Estimating the degree of multinationality has led to a choice of different measures. From an examination of the literature, Sullivan[9] identified three attributes of the degree of multinationality:

1. *Performance*—in terms of what goes on overseas[10]

2. *Structure*—in terms of what resources are used overseas[11]

3. *Attitude or conduct*—in terms of what is top management orientation[12]

In terms of performance, four measures have been used to operationalize multinationality: (1) foreign sales as a percentage of total sales (FSTS),[13] (2) research and development intensity (RDI),[14] (3) advertising intensity (AI),[15] and (4) foreign profits as a percentage of total profits (FPTP).

In terms of structure, two measures of multinationality have been used: (1) foreign assets/total assets (FATA) and (2) overseas subsidiaries as percentage of total subsidiaries (OSTS).[16]

In terms of attitude, two measures of multinationality have been used: (1) top management's international experience (TMIE) as the cumulative duration of top management's international assignments weighted by the reported total of work experience of the top management team of the firm,[17] and (2) the psychic dispersion of international operations (PAIO).[18]

Of these eight measures, those based on foreign revenue, foreign assets, and foreign revenues are the only ones that are accounting based and mandated by SFAS No. 14. They are chosen for this study as accounting-based measures of multinationality available to the market through the mandated disclosures of SFAS No. 14.

In the rest of this chapter we discuss methodology and hypothesis development, the research method, and the analytical test and results.

METHODOLOGY AND HYPOTHESIS DEVELOPMENT

The methodology for the analysis builds on the relationship between the market value of equity and balance sheet or profit and loss statement information. The most popular thesis identifies a positive relationship between annual market value of equity and one of the following items of accounting information: (a) total earnings, (b) total assets, and (c) total revenues. As such it may be referred to as an association study. It may be expressed as follows.

$$MVv_{it} = a_0 + a_1 TP_{it} + e_{1it} \quad (1)$$
$$MV_{it} = b_0 + b_1 TA_{it} + e_{2it} \quad (2)$$
$$MV_{it} = c_0 + c_1 TR_{it} + e_{3it} \quad (3)$$

where:

MV_{it} = Market value of equity for firm i for period t

TP_{it} = Total profit of a firm i for period t

TR_{it} = Total revenues for firm i for period t

The decomposition of equations (1), (2), and (3) into domestic and foreign components based upon GAAP and the deflation by book value of equity leads to the following respecification of the three equations:

$$MV_{it} = a_0' + a_1' FP_{it} + a_2' DP_{it} + e_{2it}' \quad (4)$$
$$MV_{it} = b_0' + b_1' FA_{it} + b_2' DA_{it} + e_{2it}' \quad (5)$$
$$MV_{it} = c_0' + c_1' FR_{it} + c_2' DP_{it} + e_{2it}' \quad (6)$$

where:

FP_{it} = Foreign profits for firm i in period t

DP_{it} = Domestic profits for firm i in period t

FA_{it} = Foreign assets for firm i in period t

DA_{it} = Domestic assets for firm i in period t

FR_{it} = Foreign revenues for firm i in period t

DR_{it} = Domestic revenues for firm i in period t

Both dependent and independent variables are deflated by the book value of equity.

The decomposition allows us to examine the three questions about the valuation of multinationality of U.S. multinational firms using accounting-based measures of multinationality derived from SFAS No. 14 mandated accounting information. First, are levels in domestic and foreign components of either earnings, assets, or revenues associated with the level of the market value of the firm? This question examines whether the market incorporates the domestic and foreign components of either earnings, assets, or revenues when valuing the firm and involves testing (1) $a_1' = 0$ and $a_2' = 0$, (2) $b_1' = 0$ and $b_2' = 0$, and (3) $c_1' = 0$ and $c_2' = 0$. Second, which foreign components provide the highest association? This question examines whether the market attaches higher values to the foreign and domestic components of either profits, assets, or revenues and involves comparing the coefficient of determination obtained by each of equations (4), (5), and (6). Third, are the domestic and foreign components of earnings assets or revenues capitalized by the market at the same rate? This involves testing the null hypotheses that (1) $a_1' = a_2'$, (2) $b_1' = b_2'$, and (3) $c_1' = c_2'$. The last research question can easily lead to the favored argument that foreign earnings, assets, or revenues will be less highly valued than the domestic counterparts given their high unreliability, uncertainty, and riskiness.[19] An argument that deserves to be investigated and that may explain the larger domestic association coefficients relates to the differential corporate reputation perceived by the market in foreign versus domestic operations. To create the right impression or reputation, firms signal their key characteristics to constituents to maximize their social status.[20] Basically, corporate audiences were found to construct reputations on the basis of accounting and market information or signal regarding firm performance.[21-23] These reputations have become established and constitute signals that may affect the actions of firms' stakeholders, including their shareholders. Since foreign operations generally represent a minority of most U.S. firms' total operations, these corporate reputations are created more by the domestic operations that the foreign operations. We should expect a larger association between the market value of a firm and domesticity than multinationality for firms with high corporate reputation.

RESEARCH METHOD

In this study the associations between annual market value and three different accounting-based measures of multinationality, both deflated by book value of equity, are presented as evidence of the relevance of multinationality. To describe and assess the significance of the relationship, we use three linear regression approaches (Models 4 and 6) that relate market value deflated by book value of equity to measures of multinationality and domesticity deflated by book value of equity and derived from a decomposition of earnings, total assets, and revenues into foreign and domestic components.

Sample Selection

The population consists of firms included in both *Forbes'* Most International 100 American manufacturing and service firms and *Fortune's* surveys of corporate reputation from 1986 to 1990. The security data are collected from the CRSP return files. The accounting variables are collected from both COMPUSTAT and the *Forbes* articles. The corporate reputation measures are collected from *Fortune's* surveys. The derivation of the corporate reputation score is explained later.

Descriptive Statistics

The initial sample examined included 423 firm-year observations that have all the market accounting and nonaccounting variables needed. To ensure that the results are not driven by outliers the step taken consists in eliminating observations for which any regression variable is more than four standard deviations from its sample mean, resulting in the reduction of the sample size by five observations. Exhibit 2.1 contains descriptive statistics and Pearson correlations of the variables used in the regressions. Note that the correlations between the domestic and the foreign components of profit, assets, and revenues deflated by book value of equity, although statistically significant, are relatively small (0.038, 0.065, and 0.099, respectively).

Exhibit 2.1
Summary Statistics for Empirical Variables

Panel A: Distributional Characteristics (In millions)

Variables	Mean	Standard Deviations	Maximum	75%	Median	75%	Minimum
FP/BVE	2.516	13.44	171.28	0.1072	0.076	0.034	0.018
FA/BVE	231.53	1233	25406	1.1524	0.801	0.547	0.166
FR/BVE	36.31	186.32	2888	1.448	0.976	0.668	0.325
DP/BVE	2.84	13.39	126.60	0.165	0.106	0.057	0.023
DA/BVE	440.13	1951	20920	2.925	1.836	1.391	0.459
DR/BVE	67.42	278.97	2730	3.026	1.914	1.284	1.011
MV/BVE	48.46	186.31	67.71	3.702	2.081	1.418	1.062

Panel B: Pearson Correlations Among Regression Variables

	FP/BVE	FA/BVE	FR/BVE	DP/BVE	DA/BVE	DR/BVE	MV/BVE
FP/BVE	1.000						
FA/BVE	0.925[a]	1.000					
FR/BVE	0.903[a]	0.962[a]					
DP/BVE	0.038[a]	0.758[a]	0.766[a]	1.000			
DA/BVE	0.837[a]	0.065[a]	0.843[a]	0.796[a]	1.000		
DR/BVE	0.771[a]	0.745[a]	0.099[a]	0.842[a]	0.919[a]	1.000	
MV/BV	0.813[a]	0.746[a]	0.773[a]	0.869[a]	0.881[a]	0.845[a]	1.000

[a]Denotes *p*-value of 0.001.

Variable Definitions

FP/BVE = Foreign profit deflated by book value of equity
FA/BVE = Foreign assets deflated by book value of equity
FR/BVE = Foreign revenues deflated by book value of equity
DP/BVE = Domestic profit deflated by book value of equity
DA/BVE = Domestic assets deflated by book value of equity
DR/BVE = Domestic revenues deflated by book value of equity
MV/BVE = Market value of equity deflated by book value of equity

EMPIRICAL TESTS AND RESULTS

The Association of Multinationality with Market Value

Exhibit 2.2 presents the regression results for Models 4 to 6. The models relate the market value of equity to the domestic and foreign components of earnings (Model 4), assets (Model 5), and revenues (Model 6). As shown in Exhibit 2.2, the domesticity and multinationality coefficients are significant at the 1 percent level for the three models, indicating that the market values of U.S. multinational firms are significantly related to the domestic and foreign components of earnings, total assets, and revenues. The coefficient of determination, R^2, is the largest for Model 4 ($R^2 = 0.8194$), followed by Model 6 ($R^2 = 0.7396$) and Model 5 ($R^2 = 0.6781$). It appears from these results that multinationality as measured by foreign income provided the largest association with market value followed by those measured by revenues and assets. In the three cases the domesticity coefficient is significantly larger than the multinationality coefficient. These larger domestic association coefficients suggest that domestic earnings, assets, or revenues are capitalized at a larger rate than foreign earnings, assets, or revenues in the determination of market value.

Corporate Reputation Effects

As discussed earlier, corporate reputation is assumed to be positively related to the size of the association coefficients. A perception by the market of better corporate reputation arising from domestic operations may explain the finding of larger domestic association coefficient. To test the corporate reputation effects, the procedure adopted is to examine two groups in our sample, one of high reputation and one of low reputation, and determine whether the difference between the domestic and foreign association coefficients is different between both groups. The measurement of corporate reputation is accomplished as follows:

The *Fortune* survey covers every industry group comprising four or more companies. The industry groups are based on categories established by the U.S. Office of Management and Budget (OMB). The survey asked executives, directors, and analysts to rate a company on the following eight key attributes of representation:

Exhibit 2.2

Results of Pooled Time-Series Cross-Sectional Association Regression of Annual Market Value of Equity and Domesticity and Multinationality

	MODEL 4	MODEL 5	MODEL 6
Intercept	7.984 (1.964)[b]	14.499 (2.723)[a]	10.405 (2.191)[b]
FP/BVE	5.175 (11.796)[a]	—	—
DP/BVE	8.162 (18.528)[a]	—	—
FA/BVE	—	0.021 (2.591)[a]	—
DA/BVE	—	0.066 (12.610)[a]	—
FR/BVE	—	—	0.270 (6.517)[a]
DR/BVE	—	—	0.419 (15.204)[a]
Adjusted R^2	0.8194	0.6781	0.7396

[a]The three regressions are OLS *t*-statistics, shown in parentheses based on the White (1980) corrected standard errors.

[b]Superscripts a and b represent statistical significance at the *t* percent and 5 percent levels, respectively, for one-tailed tests.

Variable Definitions

FP/BVE = Foreign profits/book value of equity
DP/BVE = Domestic profits/book value of equity
FA/BVE = Foreign assets/book value of equity
DA/BVE = Domestic assets/book value of equity
FR/BVE = Foreign revenues/book value of equity
DR/BVE = Domestic revenues/book value of equity

1. Quality of management
2. Quality of products/service offered
3. Innovativeness
4. Value as long-term investment
5. Soundness of financial position
6. Ability to attract/develop/keep talented people
7. Responsibility to the community/environment
8. Wise use of corporate assets

Ratings were on a scale of 0 (poor) to 10 (excellent). The score met the multiple-constituency ecological model view of organization and effectiveness. For purposes of this study the 1986 to 1990 *Fortune* magazine surveys were used. To obtain a unique configuration, a factor analysis is used to isolate the factor common to the eight measures of reputation. All the observations were subjected to factor analysis and one common factor was found to explain the intercorrelations among the eight individual measures. Exhibit 2.3 reports the results of the common factor analysis. One common factor appears to explain the intercorrelations among the eight variables, as the first eigenvalue alone exceeds the sum of the commonalities. The common factor is significantly and positively correlated with the eight measures. Based on the factor scores, high representation firms were chosen from the top 25 percent of the distribution factor scores and low representation firms were chosen from the bottom 25 percent of the distribution factor scores.

Exhibit 2.4 presents the regression revenues for Models 4 to 6 for both a high corporate reputation group and a low corporate reputation group. As expected, in the case of the high corporate reputation group, the domestic coefficient was larger than the foreign coefficient for the three cases based on earnings, assets, and revenues. In the case of the low corporate reputation group, the foreign coefficient was the largest in the three cases. The results agree with our predictions and support our claim that corporate reputation is generated more by domestic than foreign operations.

SUMMARY AND CONCLUSIONS

This chapter investigates the association between domestic and foreign components of earnings, assets, or revenues and total annual market val-

Exhibit 2.3
Selected Statistics Related to a Common Factor Analysis of Measures of Reputation

1. Eigenvalues of the Correlation Matrix:

   Eigenvalues

1	2	3	4	5	6	7	8
6.7726	0.4596	0.3841	0.1347	0.1120	0.0549	0.0.482	0.0339

2. Factor Pattern

   FACTOR1

R_1	0.9530	R_4	0.9645	R_7	0.8072
R_2	0.9180	R_5	0.8982	R_8	0.9479
R_3	0.8789	R_6	0.9805		

3. Final Communality Estimates: Total = 1.389626

R_1	R_2	R_3	R_4	R_5	R_6	R_7	R_8
0.9083	0.8428	0.7726	0.9314	0.8069	0.9614	0.6516	0.8986

4. Standardized Scoring Coefficients

   FACTOR1

R_1	0.1407	R_4	0.1424	R_7	0.1191
R_2	0.1355	R_5	0.1326	R_8	0.1399
R_3	0.1297	R_6	0.1447		

5. Descriptive Statistics of the Common Factor Extracted from the Three Measures of Multinationality

Maximum	9.002
Third Quartile	7.288
Median	6.614
First Quartile	6.105
Minimum	3.235
Mean	6.622

Variable Definitions
R_1 = Quality of management
R_2 = Quality of products/services
R_3 = Innovativeness
R_4 = Value as long-term investment
R_5 = Soundness of financial position
R_6 = Ability to attract, develop, and keep talented people
R_7 = Responsibility to the community and environment
R_8 = Wise use of corporate assets

Exhibit 2.4
Relation between Market Value and Measures of Multinationality and Domesticity for High and Low Corporate Reputation

	Low Corporate Reputation			High Corporate Reputation		
	Model (4)	Model (5)	Model (6)	Model (4)	Model (5)	Model (6)
Intercept	5.465	19.039	9.164	3.753	10.009	13.272
	(1.601)	(2.641)	(1.611)	(1.022)		(1.476)
FP/BVE	7.049	—	—	3.688	—	—
	(17.488)			(6.147)		
DP/BVE	6.964	—	—	11.334	—	—
	(19.594)			(21.781)		
FA/BVE	—	0.085	—	—	-0.018	—
		(2.638)*			(-2.592)	
DA/BVE	—	0.070	—	—	0.1137	—
		(7.078)*			(12.969)*	
FR/BVE	—		0.3078	—		0.283
			(4.203)			(2.710)*
DR/BVE	—		0.242	—		0.558
			(9.086)			(7.626)*
Adjusted R²	0.8610	0.4934		0.9688	0.8073	0.8863

*Significant at $\alpha = 0.01$.

ues of U.S. multinational firms in the period 1986 to 1990. The results show that both measures of multinationality and domesticity have significant positive associations with the market value of equity. In the three cases examined, the association coefficient of domesticity is significantly larger than the association coefficient of multinationality especially for firms perceived to have a very good reputation. Multinationality as measured by earnings provides the largest association with market value of equity followed by revenues and assets.

NOTES

1. Financial Accounting Standards Board (FASB), *Statement of Financial Accounting Standards No. 14: Financial Reporting of Segments of a Business Enterprise* (Stanford, CT: FASB, 1976).

2. D. Sullivan, "Measuring the Degree of Internalization of a Firm," *Journal of International Business Studies* 25 (1994): 325–342.

3. J. R. Boatsman, B. K. Behn, and D. H. Patz, "A Test of the Use of Geographical Segment Disclosures," *Journal of Accounting Research* Supplement 31 (1993): 46–74.

4. G. M. Bodnar and J. Weintrop, "The Valuation of the Foreign Income of US Multinational Firms: A Growth Opportunities Perspective," *Journal of Accounting and Economics* 94 (1997): 69–97.

5. B. K. Prodhan and M. C. Harris, "Systematic Risk and the Discretionary Disclosure of Geographical Segments: An Empirical Investigation of US Multinationals," *Journal of Business, Finance, and Accounting* 16 (Autumn 1989): 467–492.

6. B. K. Prodhan, "Geographical Segment Disclosure and Multinational Risk Profile," *Journal of Business, Finance, and Accounting* 13 (Spring 1986): 15–37.

7. J. Prather-Stewart, "The Information Content of Geographic Segment Disclosure," *Advances in International Accounting* 8 (1995): 31–44.

8. H. Yang, J. Wansley, and W. Lane, "Stock Market Recognition of Multinationality of a Firm and International Events," *Journal of Business, Finance, and Accounting* 12 (1985): 263–274.

9. Sullivan, "Measuring the Degree of Internalization of a Firm."

10. J. H. Dunning, "Explaining Changing Pattern of International Production in Defense of Eclectic," *Oxford Bulletin of Economics and Statistics* 21 (1979): 269–296.

11. J. M. Stopford and L. T. Wells, *Managing the Multinational Enterprise* (New York: Basic Books, 1972).

12. H. B. Perlmutter, "The Tortuous Evaluation of the Multinational Corporation," *Columbia Journal of World Business* 4 (January-February 1969): 9–18.

13. J. D. Daniels and J. Bracker, "Profit Performance: Do Foreign Operations Make a Difference?" *Management International Review* 29, no. 1 (1989): 46–56.

14. L. Franko, "Global Corporate Competition: Who's Winning, Who's Losing, and the R&D Factor as One Reason Why," *Strategic Management Journal* 10, no. 2 (1989): 49–74.

15. R. E. Caves, *Multinational Enterprise and Economic Analysis* (Cambridge, UK: Cambridge University Press, 1982).

16. Sullivan, "Measuring the Degree of Internalization of a Firm."

17. Ibid.

18. S. Ronen and O. Shenkar, "Clustering Countries on Attitudinal Dimensions: A Review and Synthesis," *Academy of Management Review* 10, no. 3 (1985): 435–454.

19. Bodnar and Weintrop, "The Valuation of the Foreign Income of US Multinational Firms."

20. A. M. Spence, *Market Signaling: Information Transfer in Hiring and Related Screening Process* (Cambridge, MA: Harvard University Press, 1974).

21. C. Fombrum and M. Shanley, "What's in a Name? Reputational Building and Corporate Strategy," *Academy of Management Journal* 33 (1990): 233–258.

22. Ahmed Belkaoui, "Organizational Effectiveness, Social Performance and Economic Performance." *Research in Corporate Social Performance and Policy* 12 (1992): 143–155.

23. Ahmed Riahi-Belkaoui and E. Pavlik, "Asset Management Performance and Reputation Building for Large U.S. Firms," *British Journal of Management* 2 (1991): 231–238.

SELECTED READINGS

Belkaoui, Ahmed. "Organizational Effectiveness, Social Performance and Economic Performance." *Research in Corporate Social Performance and Policy* 12 (1992): 143–155.

Boatsman, J. R., B. K. Behn, and D. H. Patz. "A Test of the Use of Geographical Segment Disclosures." *Journal of Accounting Research* Supplement 31 (1993): 46–74.

Bodnar, G. M., and J. Weintrop. "The Valuation of the Foreign Income of US Multinational Firms: A Growth Opportunities Perspective." *Journal of Accounting and Economics* 94 (1997): 69–97.

Caves, R. E. *Multinational Enterprise and Economic Analysis.* Cambridge, UK: Cambridge University Press, 1982.

Daniels, J. D., and J. Bracker. "Profit Performance: Do Foreign Operations Make a Difference?" *Management International Review* 29, no. 1 (1989): 46–56.

Dunning, J. H. "Explaining Changing Pattern of International Production in Defense of Eclectic." *Oxford Bulletin of Economics and Statistics* 21 (1979): 269–296.

Financial Accounting Standards Board (FASB). *Statement of Financial Accounting Standards No. 14: Financial Reporting of Segments of a Business Enterprise.* Stamford, CT: FASB, 1976.

Fombrum, C., and M. Shanley. "What's in a Name? Reputational Building and Corporate Strategy." *Academy of Management Journal* 33 (1990): 233–258.

Franko, L. "Global Corporate Competition: Who's Winning, Who's Losing, and the R&D Factor as One Reason Why." *Strategic Management Journal* 10, no. 2 (1989): 49–74.

Perlmutter, H. B. "The Tortuous Evaluation of the Multinational Corporation." *Columbia Journal of World Business* 4 (January-February 1969): 9–18.

Prather-Stewart, J. "The Information Content of Geographic Segment Disclosure." *Advances in International Accounting* 8 (1995): 31–44.

Prodhan, B. K. "Geographical Segment Disclosure and Multinational Risk Profile." *Journal of Business, Finance, and Accounting* 13 (Spring 1986): 15–37.

Prodhan, B. K., and M. C. Harris. "Systematic Risk and the Discretionary Disclosure of Geographical Segments: An Empirical Investigation of US Multinationals." *Journal of Business, Finance, and Accounting* 16 (Autumn 1989): 467–492.

Riahi-Belkaoui, Ahmed, and E. Pavlik. "Asset Management Performance and Reputation Building for Large U.S. Firms." *British Journal of Management* 2 (1991): 231–238.

Ronen, S., and O. Shenkar. "Clustering Countries on Attitudinal Dimensions: A Review and Synthesis." *Academy of Management Review* 10, no. 3 (1985): 435–454.

Spence, A. M. *Market Signaling: Information Transfer in Hiring and Related Screening Process.* Cambridge, MA: Harvard University Press, 1974.

Stopford, J. M. and L. T. Wells. *Managing the Multinational Enterprise.* New York: Basic Books, 1972.

Sullivan, D. "Measuring the Degree of Internalization of a Firm." *Journal of International Business Studies* 25 (1994): 325–342.

White, H. A. "Heteroskedasticity-Consisent Covariance Matrix Estimator and a Direct Test for Heteroskedasticity." *Econometrika* 10 (1980): 819–838.

Yang, H., J. Wansley, and W. Lane. "Stock Market Recognition of Multinationality of a Firm and International Events." *Journal of Business, Finance, and Accounting* 12 (1985): 263–274.

The Degree of Internationalization and the Value of the Firm: Theory and Evidence

INTRODUCTION

The degree of internationalization of most large U.S. firms has reached significant levels in terms of sales, profits, and assets abroad, ranging from 10 to over 90 percent of their total operations.[1] Questions about the consequences of these large investments have focused largely on the relation between multinationality and firm performance.[2] An equally ignored and interesting research question is: What are the implications of the degree of internationalization for firm value? This chapter addresses this research question by investigating the relation between the degree of internationalization and the market value of firm equity. In contrast to previous studies, this chapter does not address the financial performance consequences to the degree of internationalization. Instead, a valuation approach is used to examine the effect of the degree of internationalization by focusing on the relation between the book value of a firm's equity and the market value of a firm's stock.

The valuation approach is used for two reasons. First, results from the financial performance effects of multinationality have been inconsistent.[3] Second, the valuation approach allows examination of the effect of multinationality on firm value by focusing on the sign of the relation between the degree of internationalization and firm value. The valuation model used in this study, proposed by Ohlson[4] and adapted by Guenther and Trombley,[5] shows the market value of the firm's equity to be a linear and stochastic function of the book value of equity, current earnings, current dividends, and the degree of internationalization. The degree of internationalization is measured by either foreign revenues over total revenues (FRTR) or foreign assets over total assets (FATA). They are by far the most used and proven variables for the measurement of multinationality. They are considered to be meaningful first-order indicators of a firm's involvement in international business.[6]

The empirical valuation model applied to the 100 largest U.S. multinational firms indicates a positive relation between the degree of internationalization and the market value of equity. It is consistent with the hypothesis of relevance of multinationality in firm valuation, whereby the degree of internationalization (DOI) is priced by the market as an unbooked intangible asset.

DEGREE OF INTERNATIONALIZATION AND FIRM VALUE

Studies examining the direction of the relationship between the degree of internationalization and the financial performance of a firm reported either a positive, indeterminate, or negative relationship. The disarray was attributed to the different measures used for both the degree of internationalization and financial performance. This study argues that the focus should be on firm value rather than financial performance however it is measured. Basically the multinational corporation is a collection of valuable options and generates arbitrage profits that enhance its value.[7] The arbitrage benefits result from (a) the exploitation of various institutional imperfections; (b) timing options; (c) technology options; and (d) staging options.[8,9] Better financing bargains,[10] as well as capital availability,[11,12] are also possible through internationalization. Whether investors recognize the enhancement of firm value through internationalization is an open research question. There is evidence indicating that investors recognize multinationality in that international firms show lower systematic risk and unsystematic risk compared to securities of purely domestic firms.[13-15] This implies that investors incorporate the degree of internationalization in determining firm value. Investors view the degree of internationalization as representing an unbooked or hidden asset, and they value it the same as those assets on the firm's balance sheet. Under this hidden asset view, the relation between the value of equity and the degree of internationalization is similar to the relation between the value of equity and other assets recorded in the firm's books. With more assets resulting in higher firm value, the hidden asset view of internationalization suggests the following hypothesis:

H: There is a positive relation between the degree of internationalization and the market value of equity.

THE EMPIRICAL MODEL

A valuation model developed by Ohlson[16] is used to provide the empirical model for the testing of the main hypothesis of the study. In Ohlson's model, the market value of equity is a linear and stochastic function of the book value of equity, current earnings, current dividends, and a variable representing other relevant factors. Ohlson's model, from Ohlson's equation (7), is as follows:

$$MV_t = k(Ox_t - d_t) + (1 - k)y_t + \&_2 v_t \tag{1}$$

where:

MV_t = market value or price of the firm at date t

$k = R_f w/(1 + R_f - w)$

R_f = the risk-free interest rate

w = persistence parameter for abnormal earnings (x^a): $x_{t+1}{}^a = wx_{at} + E_{1,t+1}$

$O_t = (R_f + 1)/R_f$

x_t = earnings for period $t-1$ to t

d_t = dividends paid at date t less new capital contributions for period $t-1$ to t

y_t = net book value at date t

$\&_2 = (R_f + 1)/(R_f + 1 - w)(R_f + 1 - y)$

v_t = a variable summarizing other information that influences the prediction of future expected abnormal earnings

y = persistence parameter for v_t: $v_{t+1} = yv_{t+1} = yv_t + E + 1$

To operationalize (1) in the empirical test of the hypothesis, the following cross-sectional OLS regression is estimated for each year:

$$MV_{it} = b_{0t} + b_{1t}(Ox_{it} - d_{it}) + b_{2t}y_{it} + b_{3t}DOI_{it} + e_{it} \qquad (2)$$

where for firm i:

P_i = market value of equity

x_i = earnings before extraordinary items

d_i = net dividends of new capital contributions

y_i = the net book value of assets

DOI = the degree of internationalization measured as either foreign revenues/total revenues (FRTR) or foreign assets/total assets(FATA)

The model allows the degree of internationalization variable *(DOI)* to be explicitly added to the model through the v_t term. In this way it is possible to test whether the degree of internationalization has value-relevant information in addition to that contained in book values of assets and earnings.

SAMPLE SELECTION AND DESCRIPTIVE STATISTICS

Since 1979, *Forbes* has annually ranked the Most International 100 American manufacturing and service firms on the basis of total foreign revenues. All the firms in *Forbes'* classification from 1987 to 1993 were included in our sample, resulting in 685 firm-year observations. The two measures of DOI were obtained from the *Forbes* data. All the other variables were obtained from the COMPUSTAT Annual Primary-Secondary-Tertiary database.

Sample descriptive statistics are presented in Exhibit 3.1.

EMPIRICAL RESULTS

OLS estimates of the coefficients of (2) are reported in Exhibit 3.2 with DOI as FRTR and Exhibit 3.3 with DOI as FATA. The results do not use any deflator but rely on White's[17] adjusted standard error estimates to deal with heteroscedasticity. The results of the pooled regression show all coefficients a_1, a_2, and a_3, to be significant and positive. The

Exhibit 3.1
Descriptive Statistics

Variable	Notation	Mean	Standard Deviation	Medium
Foreign Revenue/ Total Revenue	$FRTR_{ir}$	38.4535	16.8624	37.70
Foreign Assets/ Total Assets	$FATA_{it}$	39.9212	202.1856	30.50
Earnings Before Extraordinary				
Items (million)	X_{it}	769.7911	1199.824	543
Total Assets	TA_{it}	99626.38	43942.55	10335.5
Equity	Y_{it}	4898.299	6658.825	2984.98
Market Value	MV_{it}	11483.85	13486.81	6884

results on a_1 and a_2 present a confirmation of the Ohlson model. The results on a_3 in both Exhibit 3.2 and 3.3 provide a confirmation of the hypothesis that there is a positive relation between the degree of internationalization and the market value of the firm. The results of the annual regressions confirm the stability of the Ohlson model and the positive relation between DOI and the market value of the firm. The nonsignificant intercepts in Exhibit 3.2 and for most years in Exhibit 3.3 suggest that no value-relevant variables are omitted from the model. To determine whether these results are sensitive to the choice of a deflator, the OLS estimates of the coefficients of (2) after deflating all the variables by total assets are shown in Exhibits 3.4 and 3.5. The results confirm the previous findings with nondeflated data.

SUMMARY AND CONCLUSIONS

This chapter investigates the effect of the degree of internationalization on the relation between the book value and market value of equity of the Most International 100 manufacturing and service firms. The hypothesis of a positive relation between the degree of internationalization and the market value of a firm is confirmed by our results, adding credence to the "hidden asset" view of internationalization. Basically, the

Exhibit 3.2
Estimated Coefficients (t-Values) for Pooled and Annual Regression of the Valuation Model

$$MV_{it} = a_{0t} + a_{1t}(Ox_{it} - d_{it}) + a_{2t}y_{it} + a_{3t}FRTR_{it} + e_{it}$$

Y	n	a_0	a_1	a_2	a_3	Adj. R^2
1987	98	-1571.84 (-1.189)	1.1407 (10.169)*	1.1195 (16.379)*	89.403 (2.559)*	0.7943
1988	96	-179.95 (-0.137)	1.1780 (11.174)*	1.1857 (18.624)*	53.348 (1.659)*	0.7894
1989	100	932.566 (0.527)	1.3118 (8.909)*	1.2407 (14.355)*	61.03 (1.901)*	0.6776
1990	95	-1520.35 (-0.685)	1.49212 (8.201)*	1.314 (12.90)*	94.4263 (1.844)*	0.6545
1991	97	608.4287 (-0.220)	1.9534 (8.433)*	1.6085 (11.515)*	83.638 (1.299)	0.5824
1992	100	-136.022 (-0.049)	2.1752 (9.403)*	1.7573 (12.843)*	63.1574 (1.065)	0.6197
1993	99	358.4708 (0.133)	9.6247 (10.099)*	2.2348 (12.959)	22.0475 (0.396)	0.6263
1987-1993	685	-107.118 (-0.184)	1.9227 (15.907)	1.3791 (30.216)*	70.5309 (3.985)*	0.6501

*Significant at the 0.01 level.
Variable Definitions
MV   = market value of equity
O   = $(1 + R_f)/R_f$ where R_f is the average annual rate of return in 30-day treasury securities
x   = net income before extraordinary items
d   = dividends net of new capital contribution (change in common equity minus net income)
y   = book value of common equity
FRTR = foreign revenue/total revenue

degree of internationalization is priced by the market as if it were an additional unbooked asset of the firm.

The study implies that investors value multinationality in pricing the equities of multinational firms as an important and relevant variable. The degree of internationalization appears as useful in the valuation of equities of multinational firms as published accounting information. The results are useful not only to investors but also to standard setters. If

Exhibit 3.3
Estimated Coefficients (*t*-Values) for Pooled and Annual Regression of the Valuation Model

$$MV_{it} = a_{0t} + a_{1t}(Ox_{it} - d_{it}) + a_{2t}y_{it} + a_{3t}FATA_{it} + e_{it}$$

Y	n	a_0	a_1	a_2	a_3	Adj. R^2
1987	96	-394.965 (-0.485)	3.6904 (6.643)*	0.7183 (6.585)*	37.2764 (4.78)*	0.7831
1988	94	-80.355 (-0.10)	4.2889 (4.999)*	0.6375 (4.922)*	45.2962 (3.694)*	0.8095
1989	98	1074.65 (1.181)	5.2247 (6.072)*	0.6555 (4.379)*	55.4607 (4.661)*	0.7291
1990	95	-1493.49 (-1.853)*	7.2791 (12.301)	0.6127 (6.083)*	79.9790 (10.086)*	0.8253
1991	95	147.656 (0.125)	6.1156 (9.417)*	1.2854 (10.115)*	55.7794 (6.794)*	0.7149
1992	97	-60.858 (-0.051)	5.7630 (10.362)	1.5018 (12.569)*	48.3236 (6.964)*	0.7442
1993	95	1031.598 (0.70)	3.4037 (4.871)*	2.0772 (9.965)*	12.061 (1.299)	0.6258
1987-1993	670	1036.13 (2.356)	4.7714 (15.607)	1.0852 (20.147)*	36.735 (9.546)*	0.6437

*Significant at the 0.01 level.
**Significant at the 0.05 level.
Variable Definitions
MV = market value of equity
O = $(1 + R_f)/R_f$ where R_f is the average annual rate of return in 30-day treasury securities
x = net income before extraordinary items
d = dividend net of new capital contribution (change in common equity minus net income)
y = book value of common equity
FATA = foreign assets/total assets

multinationality is a key variable in the market valuation of equity, it constitutes an unbooked and intangible asset of the firm and ought to be given a disclosure treatment. Whether the disclosure of the level of multinationality should be mandated or not is not an issue. The realization that it is a key determinant of the value of the firm ought to convince firms of the appropriateness of some form of disclosure. These impli-

Exhibit 3.4
Estimated Coefficients and *t*-Values for Pooled Regression of Assets-Deflated
Ohlson Valuation Model with *DOI=FRTR*

$MV_{it} = a_{0t} + a_{1t}(Ox_{it} - d_{it}) + b_2 y_{it} + a_3 FRTR_{it} + e_{it}$

Variable	Coefficient	Standard Error	*t*-Statistic	Probability
constant	-0.6592	0.0299	-21.978	0.0001
b1	4.4096	0.0322	136.696	0.0001
b2	3.5365	0.0276	127.730	0.0001
b3	25.9697	4.19	6.188	0.0001

$N = 641$, adjusted $R^2 = 0.75$
See Exhibit 3.2 for variable definitions.

Exhibit 3.5
Estimated Coefficients and *t*-Values for Pooled Regression of Assets-Deflated
Valuation Model with *DOI=FATA*

$$MV_{it} = a_{0t} + a_{1t}(Ox_{it} - d_{it}) + a_2 y_{it} + a_3 FATA_{it} + e_{it}$$

Variable	Coefficient	Standard Error	*t*-Statistic	Probability
constant	-0.5652	0.0270	-20.868	0.0001
b1	6.4057	0.1757	36.448	0.0001
b2	2.7205	0.0965	28.173	0.0001
b3	36.2010	3.54.7	10.229	0.0001

$N = 629$, adjusted $R^2 = 0.76$
See Exhibit 3.3 for variable definitions.

cations call for more research on the market valuation of multinationality. Future research needs to consider different time periods, a different sample of companies, and different market valuation models.

NOTES

1. Ahmed Riahi-Belkaoui, *International and Multinational Accounting* (London, UK: Dryden Press, 1994).

2. Daniel Sullivan, "Measuring the Degree of Internationalization of a Firm," *Journal of International Business Studies* 25 (1994): 325–342.

3. Ibid.

4. J. Ohlson, "Earnings, Book Values, and Dividends in Security Valuation," Working Paper (New York: Columbia University, 1991).

5. David A. Guenther and Mark A. Trombley, "The 'LIFO Reserve' and the Value of the Firm: Theory and Evidence," *Contemporary Accounting Research* 10 (1994): 433–452.

6. Sullivan, "Measuring the Degree of Internationalization of a Firm," 325–342.

7. George P. Tsetsekos, "Multinationality and Common Stock Offering," *Journal of International Financial Management and Accounting* 3 (1991): 1–16.

8. C. Baldwin, "The Capital Factor: Competing for Capital in Global Environment." In M. Porter, ed. *Competition in Global Industries* (Boston: Harvard Business School Press, 1986): 184–223.

9. B. Kogut, "Foreign Direct Investment as a Sequential Process." In C. P. Kindelberger and D. B. Audretsch, eds. *The Multinational Corporation in the 1980s* (Cambridge, MA: MIT Press, 1993): 38–56.

10. F. Giavazzi and A. Giovannini, *Limiting Exchange Rate Flexibility: The European Monetary System* (Cambridge, MA: MIT Press, 1989).

11. D. Eiteman and A. Stonehill, *Multinational Business Finance* (Boston: Addison-Wesley, 1986).

12. A. Shapiro, *Multinational Financial Management*, 3d ed. (Boston: Allyn & Bacon, 1989).

13. T. Agmon and D. R. Lessard, "Investor Recognition of Corporate International Diversification," *Journal of Finance* (1977): 1049–1055.

14. V. Errunza and L. Senbert, "The Effects of International Corporate Diversification, Market Valuation and Size Adjusted Evidence," *Journal of Finance* 11 (1981): 717–743.

15. H. Yang, J. Wansley, and W. Lane, "Stock Market Recognition of Multinationality of a Firm and International Events," *Journal of Business Finance and Accounting* 12 (1985): 263–274.

16. Ohlson, "Earnings, Book Values, and Dividends in Security Valuation."

17. H. A. White, "Heteroskedasticity-Consistent Covariance Matrix Estimator and a Direct Test for Heteroskedasticity," *Econometrika* 10 (1980): 817–838.

SELECTED READINGS

Agmon, T., and D. R. Lessard, "Investor Recognition of Corporate International Diversification." *Journal of Finance* (1977): 1049–1055.

Baldwin, C. "The Capital Factor: Competing for Capital in Global Environment." In M. Porter, ed. *Competition in Global Industries*. Boston: Harvard Business School Press, 1986: 184–223.

Eiteman, D., and A. Stonehill. *Multinational Business Finance*. Boston: Addison-Wesley, 1986.

Errunza, V., and L. Senbert. "The Effects of International Corporate Diversification, Market Valuation and Size Adjusted Evidence." *Journal of Finance* 11 (1981): 717–743.

Giavazzi, F., and A. Giovannini. *Limiting Exchange Rate Flexibility: The European Monetary System*. Cambridge, MA: MIT Press, 1989.

Guenther, David A., and Mark A. Trombley. "The 'LIFO Reserve' and the Value of the Firm: Theory and Evidence." *Contemporary Accounting Research* 10 (1994): 433–452.

Kogut, B. "Foreign Direct Investment as a Sequential Process." In C. P. Kindelberger and D. B. Audretsch, eds. *The Multinational Corporation in the 1980s*. Cambridge, MA: MIT Press, 1993: 38–56.

Ohlson, J. "Earnings, Book Values, and Dividends in Security Valuation." Working Paper. New York: Columbia University, 1991.

Riahi-Belkaoui, Ahmed. *International and Multinational Accounting*. London: Dryden Press, 1994.

Shapiro, A. *Multinational Financial Management*, 3d ed. Boston: Allyn & Bacon, 1989.

Sullivan, Daniel. "Measuring the Degree of Internationalization of a Firm." *Journal of International Business Studies* 25 (1994): 325–342.

Tsetsekos, George P. "Multinationality and Common Stock Offering." *Journal of International Financial Management and Accounting* 3 (1991): 1–16.

White, H. A. "Heteroskedasticity-Consistent Covariance Matrix Estimator and a Direct Test for Heteroskedasticity." *Econometrika* 10 (1980): 817–838.

Yang, H., J. Wansley, and W. Lane, "Stock Market Recognition of Multinationality of a Firm and International Events." *Journal of Business Finance and Accounting* 12 (1985): 263–274.

4
_____

The Value-Relevance of Earnings, Cash Flows, Multinationality, and Corporate Reputation as Assessed by Securing Market Effects

INTRODUCTION

This chapter assesses the value-relevance of required earnings and cash flows from operations disclosures by firms and multinationality and corporate reputation measures disclosed outside the required accounting reports. We focus on key accounting and nonaccounting dimensions of relevance to individual investor and the investment community at large—whether earnings and cash flows from operations as mandated disclosures in annual reports and multinationality and corporate reputation as voluntary disclosures outside the annual reports by both *Forbes* magazine and *Fortune* magazine are associated with market valuations of business enterprises. In assessing value-relevance, we examine incremental stock price effects for multinationality and corporate reputation beyond both earnings and cash flows from operations.

The individual investor is generally interested in nonaccounting information that can reinforce expectations formed by earnings and cash flow disclosures. By examining equity market reaction to multinationality and corporate reputation made available annually by *Forbes* and *Fortune*, the chapter provides individual investors with evidence concerning the importance of these data with respect to market valuation.

The investment community at large is also interested in nonaccounting information if it contributes to an effective allocation of capital and to the efficiency of the capital markets.[1] An analysis of firms' security prices should reveal the relevance of multinationality and corporate reputation for market valuation. A significant association will show that the disclosure of multinationality and corporate reputation, in addition to earnings and cash flows, contributes to effective allocation of capital by enabling investors and creditors to identify the most profitable firms.

A vast amount of firm data can be communicated to users and market participants. Policymakers must decide which data need to be mandated as useful for efficient risk sharing and allocation of scarce resources. In addition to earnings and cash flows from operations that are mandated, multinationality and corporate reputation are voluntarily provided by *Forbes* and *Fortune*. The value-relevance of these two items of nonaccounting information constitutes an excellent input to the FASB about the need to disclose in annual reports information on both multinationality and corporate reputation.

Our study addresses two issues. We first examine whether cash flows from operations disclosures required by SFAS No. 95 *Statement of Cash Flows*[2] has incremental value-relevance beyond accounting-based accounting earnings in explaining security market returns. The results will add to numerous studies examining whether, in addition to earnings, the disclosure of cash flow from operations leads to additional value-relevant information. The focus in this study is on cash flow from operations rather than the other two main cash flow components reported in the financial statements, i.e., cash flows from investing activities and cash flow from financing activities. As argued by Cheng et al.,[3] the rate of return measure used captures continuing operating activities rather than the cash effects from investing and financing activities.

The second issue concerns the incremental firm value effects of multinationality and corporate reputation disclosed by *Forbes* and *Fortune* magazines.

The next section discusses incremental firm value effects of cash-flows from operations and accrual accounting earnings. The third and fourth sections discuss respectively the firm value effects of multinationality and corporate reputation. The fifth section describes the research method used to assess the relationships between earnings, cash flows, multinationality, corporate reputation, and firm value, followed by the empirical results of this analysis. The final section provides a summary and concluding remarks.

EARNINGS, CASH FLOWS, AND EQUITY VALUATION

Accounting research, since the late 1960s, has provided ample evidence of the significant effects of accounting earnings disclosures on firms' security prices.[4-6] Earnings appear to affect equity prices, even though the effect is in some cases small. Given, however, the constant criticism levied at earnings because of its historical emphasis, or because it may be subject to earnings management, research has focused on the incremental value-relevance of cash flows from operations, both estimate of cash flows from pre-SFAS No. 95 *Statement of Cash Flows*[7] and SFAS No. 95 data.[8-14] To test for incremental associations between security returns and reported cash flows, after controlling for earnings, the following linear regression model is generally used.[15]

$$R_{jt} = \alpha_{0t} + \alpha_{1t}\Delta E_{jt}/MV_{jt-1} + \alpha_{2t}E_{jt}/MV_{jt-1}$$
$$+ \alpha_3\Delta CF_{jt}/MV_{jt-1} + \alpha_{4t}CF_{jt}/MV_{jt-1} + E_{jt} \qquad (1)$$

where:

R_{jt} = Change in the market value for firm j in year t

$\quad = \dfrac{MV_{jt} - MV_{jt-1}}{MV_{jt}}$

MV_{jt} = Market value of firm j at the end of year t

E_{jt} = Earnings for firm j in year t

CF_{jt} = Cash flows from operations for firm j in year t

ΔE_{jt} = Changes in earnings for firm j in year t

ΔCF_{jt} = Changes in cash flows for firm j in year t

Model 1 uses both the change and level forms for earnings and cash flows from operations as suggested by various studies.[16,17] The sum of the change and level coefficients for earnings ($\alpha_{1t} + \alpha_{2t}$) and for cash flows ($\alpha_{3t} + \alpha_{4t}$) are, respectively, the earnings response coefficient and the cash flows from operations response coefficient. They can be used to assess, respectively, the value-relevance of earnings and the value-relevance of cash flows.[18-20]

MULTINATIONALITY AND EQUITY VALUATION

Studies examining the direction of the relationship between multinationality and the financial performance of a firm reported either a positive, indeterminate, or negative relationship. The disarray was attributed to the different measures used for both the degree of internationalization and financial performance. This study argues that the focus should be on firm value rather than financial performance however it is measured. Basically, the multinational corporation is a collection of valuable options and generates arbitrage profits that enhance its value.[21] The arbitrage benefits result from (a) the exploitation of various institutional imperfections; (b) timing options; (c) technology options; and (d) staging options.[22,23] Better financing bargains,[24] as well as capital availability,[25,26] are also possible through internationalization. Whether investors recognize the enhancement of firm value through internationalization is an open research question. There is evidence indicating that investors recognize multinationality in that international firms show lower systematic risk and unsystematic risk compared to securities of purely domestic firms.[27-29] This implies that investors incorporate the degree of internationalization in determining firm value.[30] Investors view the degree of internationalization as representing an unbooked or hidden asset, and they value it the same as those assets on the firm's balance sheet. Under this hidden asset view, the relation between the value of equity and the degree of internationalization is similar to the relation between the value of equity and other assets recorded in the firm's books. With more productive assets resulting in higher firm value, the hidden asset view of internationalization suggests a positive relation between the degree of internationalization or multinationality and the market value of equity.

To test the incremental associations between security returns and multinationality, after controlling for earnings and cash flow, Model 1 is adjusted as follows:

$$
\begin{aligned}
R_{jt} = \ &\alpha_{0t} + \alpha_{1t}\Delta E_{jt}/MV_{jt-1} + \alpha_{2t}E_{jt}/MV_{jt-1} + \alpha_{3t}\Delta CF_{jt}/MV_{jt-1} \\
&+ \alpha_{4t}CF_{jt}/MV_{jt-1} + \alpha_{5t}MULT_{jt} + E_{2jt}
\end{aligned} \tag{2}
$$

where:

$MULT_{jt}$ = level of multinationality of firm j for year t

REPUTATION AND EQUITY VALUATION

The reputation of a firm is important for various decisions ranging from resource allocation and career decisions to product choices, to name only a few.[31] It is an important signal of the firm's organizational effectiveness. Favorable reputations can create favorable situations for firms that include: (1) the generation of excess returns by inhibiting the mobility of rivals in an industry[32]; (2) the capability of charging premium prices to consumers[33]; and (3) the creation of a better image in the capital markets and to investors.[34] To create the right impression or reputation, firms signal their key characteristics to constituents to maximize their social status.[35] In fact, corporate audiences were found to construct reputations on the basis of accounting and market information or signals regarding firm performance.[36-38] These reputations have become established and constitute signals that may affect the actions of firms' stakeholders, including their shareholders. Specifically, a good reputation can be construed as a competitive advantage within an industry.[39] This implies that investors incorporate reputation in determining firm value, which suggests a positive relationship between firm value and corporate reputation.

To test for incremental association between security returns and corporate reputation, after controlling for earnings, cash flows, and multinationality, Model 2 is adjusted as follows:

$$R_{jt} = \alpha_{0t} + \alpha_{1t}\Delta E_{jt}/MV_{jt-1} + \alpha_{2t}E_{jt}/MV_{jt-1} + \alpha_{3t}\Delta CF_{jt}/MV_{jt-1}$$
$$+ \alpha_{4t}CF_{jt}/MV_{jt-1} + \alpha_{5t}MULT_{jt} + \alpha_{6t}CR_{jt} + E_{3jt} \qquad (3)$$

where:

CR_{jt} = Corporate reputation score for firm j in year t

CONDITIONING AND THE ANALYSIS ON MACROECONOMIC VARIABLES

As in previous studies,[40-43] the value-relevance of earnings, cash flows, multinationality, and corporate reputation is conducted in a conditioned (contextual) mode. We extend the analysis to allow for different economic conditions as important in the relationship between firm value on one hand, and earnings, cash flows, multinationality, and corporate reputation on the other hand. Three economic variables were chosen for the contextual analysis: (a) the index of business formation (a business activity indicator), (b) the annual change in the Consumer Price Index (an inflation indicator), and (c) the annual change in real GNP (a state-of-the-economy variable). The final model is as follows:

$$R_{jt} = \alpha_{0t} + \alpha_{1t}\Delta E_{jt}/MV_{jt-1} + \alpha_{2t}E_{jt}/MV_{jt-1} + \alpha_{3t}\Delta CF_{jt}/MV_{jt-1}$$
$$+ \alpha_{4t}CF_{jt}/MV_{jt-1} + \alpha_{5t}MULT_{jt} + \alpha_{6t}CR_{jt} + \alpha_{7t}ION_t$$
$$+ \alpha_{8t}INF_t + I_{gt}GNP_t + E_{4jt} \tag{4}$$

where:

ION_t = Index of business formation for year t

INF_t = Annual change in the Consumer Price Index for year t

GNP_t = Annual change in real GNP for year t

RESEARCH METHOD

In this study, incremental associations between security return measures and cash flow from operations, multinationality, and corporate reputation, after controlling for earnings and conditioning the analysis to include the macroeconomic variables of index of business formation, annual change in Consumer Price Index, and annual change in real GNP, are presented as evidence of the relevance of these accounting and non-accounting disclosures. To describe and assess the significance of those relationships, we use four linear regression approaches (Models 1 to 4) that relate changes in market value to the accounting and nonaccounting variables mentioned earlier and to the macroeconomic variables.

Data and Sample Selection

The population consists of firms included in both *Forbes'* Most International 100 American manufacturing and service firms and *Fortune's* surveys of corporate reputation from 1987 to 1993. The security data are collected from the CRSP Return files. The accounting variables are collected from COMPUSTAT. Earnings is income before extraordinary items (COMPUSTAT data item 18). Cash flows from operations are reported under SFAS No. 95 (COMPUSTAT data item 308). The macroeconomic variables, ION, INF, and GNP are collected from the *Economic Report of the President*.[44] The derivation of the multinationality and corporate reputation variables is explained later. The final sample includes 395 firm-year observations that have all the accounting and nonaccounting variables over the period of analysis.

Measuring Multinationality

Previous research has attempted to measure the following attributes of multinationality:

1. *Performance*—in terms of what goes on overseas[45]

2. *Structure*—in terms of resources used overseas[46]

3. *Attitude or Conduct*—in terms of what is top management's orientation[47]

Sullivan[48] developed nine measures of which five were shown to have a high reliability in the construction of a homogeneous measure of nationality: (1) foreign sales as a percentage of total sales (FSTS), (2) foreign assets over total assets (FATA), (3) overseas subsidiaries as a percentage of total subsidiaries (OSTS), (4) top management's international experience (TMIE), and (5) psychic dispersion of international operations (PDIO).

In this study we follow a similar approach by measuring multinationality through three measures: (1) foreign sales/total sales (FSTS), (2) foreign profits/total profits (FPTP), and (3) foreign assets/total assets (FATA).

Descriptive statistics and correlations among the three multinationality measures are shown in Exhibit 4.1. Correlations among the variables are positive and, with one exception, all significant. The nonsignificant correlation is between FPTP and FATA. The low correlations between FPTP, FSTS, and FATA indicate that each variable can make a unique contribution as a multinationality measure. Thus, a factor analysis of all observations is used to isolate the factor common to the three measures. Exhibit 4.2 reports the results. One common factor appears in the intercorrelations among the three variables, as the first eigenvalue alone exceeds the sum of the commonalities. The common factor is significantly positively correlated with the three measures. These factors' scores were used to measure the degree of multinationality of firms in the sample.

Exhibit 4.1
Descriptive Statistics and Correlations of Three Measures of
Multinationality for *Forbes'* The Most International 100 U.S. Firms

Panel A: Descriptive Statistics

	FP/TP[a]	FS/TS[b]	FA/TA[c]
Maximum	914.3	93	91
Third Quartile	61.9	47.4	41.4
Median	41.3	36.7	30.5
First Quartile	25	25.7	22.6
Minimum	0.2	6.6	2.7
Mean	52.81	37.45	39.92

Panel B: Correlations

	FT/TP	FS/TS	FA/TA
FP/TP	1.000		
FS/TS	0.280	1.000	
FA/TA	0.034	0.193*	1.000

[a]FP/TP = Foreign profits/total profits
[b]FS/TS = Foreign sales/total sales
[c]FA/TA = Foreign assets/total assets
*Denotes p-value < 0.05.

Measuring Corporate Reputation

The independent variable of reputation is the combined score obtained in an annual *Fortune* magazine. The *Fortune* survey covers every industry group comprising four or more companies. The industry groups are based on categories established by the U.S. Office of Management and Budget (OMB). The survey asked executives, directors, and analysts to rate a company on the following eight key attributes of reputation:

1. Quality of management
2. Quality of products/service offered
3. Innovativeness
4. Value as a long-term investment
5. Soundness of financial position

Exhibit 4.2
Selected Statistics Related to a Common Factor Analysis of Three Measures of Multinationality for *Forbes'* The Most International 100 U.S. Firms

1. Eigenvalues of the Correlation Matrix:

Eigenvalues	1	2	3
	1.3615	0.9680	0.6705

2. Factor Pattern

    FACTOR 1

	FS/TS	FP/TP	FA/TA
	0.80529	0.50172	0.67918

3. Final Communality Estimates: Total = 1.361489

	FS/TS	FP/TP	FA/TA
	0.648491	0.251718	0.461280

4. Standardized Scoring Coefficients

    FACTOR 2

	FS/TS	FP/TP	FA/TA
	0.59148	0.36850	0.49885

5. Descriptive Statistics of the Common Factor Extracted from the Three Measures of Multinationality

Maximum	2039.24
Third Quartile	74.70
Median	57.03
First Quartile	40.76
Minimum	5.17
Mean	64.35

6. Ability to attract/develop/keep talented people

7. Responsibility to the community/environment

8. Wise use of corporate assets

Ratings were on a scale of 0 (poor) to 10 (excellent). The score met the multiple-consistency ecological model view of organization effectiveness. For the purpose of our study, the 1987 to 1993 *Fortune* magazine surveys were used. The use of the overall score rather than factor analysis of the eight scores is based on the facts that: (a) it is the overall score that is published in *Fortune* magazine rather than the eight scores on the attribute, and (b) it is then the overall score that is perceived by the readers as well as the respondents of the survey as the reputation index. From previous experience, the respondents know that the means of their scores on the eight attributes will be published as the overall score of reputation.

RESULTS

Panel A of Exhibit 4.3 reports description statistics for the variables used in our tests and panel B shows correlations among variables. The mean values of 0.1694 for cash flows over beginning market value and 0.0313 for change in cash flows are similar to the values used in other studies.[49,50]

The correlation reported in panel B of Exhibit 4.1 show that all correlations between R_{jt}, $\Delta E_{jt}/MV_{jt-1}$, E_{jt}/MV_{jt-1}, $\Delta CF_{jt}/MV_{jt-1}$, and CF_{jt}/MV_{jt-1} are significant at the 0.01 level. The significant associations among the accounting variables indicate some degree of collinearity among the independent variables in the regressions analyses. However, the maximum conditions index in all subsequent regression with earnings and both cash flow variables is only 4.43. As suggested by Belsley et al.,[51] mild collinearity is diagnosed for maximum condition indices between 5 and 10 and severe collinearity for an index over 30. Thus, collinearity does not seem to influence results.

For each of the multivariate regressions to be reported, we performed additional specification tests, including checks for normality and consideration of various scatter plots. A null hypothesis of normality could not be rejected at the 0.01 level in all cases, and the plots revealed some heteroscedasticity but no other obvious problems. Therefore, we calcu-

Exhibit 4.3
Descriptive Statistics and Correlations[a]

Panel A: Descriptive Statistics

Variables	Mean	Standard Derivation	Minimum	25%	Median	75%	Max
R_{jt}	0.4244	0.4389	-0.9277	-0.1417	0.0630	0.2744	7.3141
$\Delta E_{jt}/MV_{jt-1}$	0.0279	0.4088	-0.8179	-0.0252	0.0082	0.0248	7.1967
E_{jt}/MV_{jt-1}	0.0768	0.2567	-1.0517	0.0535	0.0770	0.1047	4.3314
$\Delta CF_{jt}/MV_{jt-1}$	0.0313	0.4030	-0.8108	-0.0304	0.0110	0.0302	6.9782
CF_{jt}/MV_{jt-1}	0.1694	0.3120	-0.5161	0.0934	0.1398	0.2081	5.5743
$MULT$	55.4858	33.3784	6.1501	37.3224	51.3302	66.3685	418.6857
CR	6.5802	0.9780	3.2275	6.0600	6.5962	7.2675	8.9787

Panel B: Correlations[b]

	R_{jt}	$\Delta E_{jt}/P_{jt-1}$	E_{jt}/P_{jt-1}	$\Delta CF_{jt}/P_{jt-1}$	CF_{jt}/P_{jt-1}	$MULT$	CR
R_{jt}							
$\Delta E_{jt}/MV_{jt-1}$	0.8932*						
E_{jt}/MV_{jt-1}	0.8457*	0.9174*					

	R_{jt}	$\Delta E_{jt}/P_{jt-1}$	E_{jt}/P_{jt-1}	$\Delta CF_{jt}/P_{jt-1}$	CF_{jt}/P_{jt-1}	$MULT$	CR
R_{jt}							
$\Delta CF_{jt}/MV_{jt-1}$	0.8821*	0.9912*	0.9073*				
CF_{jt}/MV_{jt-1}	0.8961*	0.9259*	0.9353*	0.9350*			
$MULT$	-0.0024	-0.0333	-0.0752	-0.0474	-0.0816		
CR	0.1130*	0.0649	0.1762*	0.0675	0.0774	-0.0468	

[a]Total observations: 395 firm-year observations.

[b]Pearson correlations are below the diagonal. All correlations between R_{jt}, $\Delta E_{jt}/MV_{jt-1}$, E_{jt}/MV_{jt-1}, and $\Delta CF_{jt}/MV_{jt-1}$, deflated by the market value of equity at the beginning of year t, MV_{jt-1}, are significant at the 0.01 level.

*Significant at the 0.01 level.

lated the t-statistics after correcting for heteroscedasticity in the manner described by White.[52]

Exhibit 4.4 presents the regression results for Models 1 to 4. Model 1 relates security returns to the accounting variables. As shown in Exhibit 4.2, both sets of combined coefficients—for $(\triangle E_{jt}/MV_{jt-1} + E_{jt}/MV_{jt-1})$ and $(\triangle CF_{jt}/MV_{jt-1} + CF_{jt}/MV_{jt-1})$—are significantly positive at conventional levels (≤ 0.01). As found in previous studies, earnings and cash flows from operations each provide incremental value-relevance beyond one another in explaining security returns.

Model 2 relates security returns to the accounting variables and multinationality. As shown in Exhibit 4.4, the coefficient for multinationality (0.0082) is significantly positive at a 0.01 level. In addition, R^2 increased from 81.59 percent in Model 1 to 86.67 percent in Model 2. This evidence suggests that multinationality provides incremental value-relevance beyond accounting variables in explaining security returns.

Model 3 relates security returns to the accounting variables of earnings and cash flows and the nonaccounting variables of multinationality and corporate reputation. As shown in Exhibit 4.4, the coefficient for corporate reputation (0.2592) is significantly positive at the 0.01 level. This evidence suggests that corporate reputation provides incremental value-relevance beyond accounting variables and multinationality in explaining security returns. In addition R^2 increased slightly from 86.67 percent in Model 2 to 87.05 percent in Model 3.

Model 4 presents the same result as Model 3 conditioned by macroeconomic variables. As shown in Exhibit 4.4, the coefficients for ION (0.2478) and GNP (1.170) are significantly positive while the coefficient for INF is significantly negative at conventional levels (≤ 0.01). As expected, security returns are positively related to the index of business formation and the annual change in real GNP and negatively related to the annual change in Consumer Price Index.

SUMMARY AND CONCLUSIONS

In this study, we investigated the incremental value-relevance of cash flow from operations, multinationality, and corporate reputation beyond earnings and after conditioning the analysis on macroeconomic variables. The analysis shows that cash flows from operations as required disclosure by SFAS No. 95, and multinationality and corporate reputation as nonaccounting disclosures have significant incremental explanatory power for security returns even after controlling for accounting earnings

Exhibit 4.4
Regression Results of Linear Models

	Model 1	Model 2	Model 3	Model 4
Intercept	-0.8572	-1.3586	-3.3413	-15.3253
	(8.561)*	(8.435)*	(4.545)*	(-1.831)
$(\Delta E_{jt}/MV_{jt-1} + E_{jt}/MV_{jt-1})$	1.5385	3.6336	2.5854	2.7471
	(2.349)*	(5.402)*	(3.272)*	(3.538)*
$(\Delta CF_{jt}/MV_{jt-1} + CF_{jt}/MV_{jt-1})$	5.5789	4.1102	5.0775	4.9171
	(9.184)*	(6.647)*	(7.019)*	(6.916)*
MULT	.	0.0082	0.0114	0.0114
		(3.706)*	(3.837)*	(3.895)*
CR	.	.	0.2592	0.2939
			(2.537)*	(2.918)*
ION	.	.	.	0.2478
				(2.671)*
INF	.	.	.	-0.1284
				(-4.531)*
GNP	.	.	.	1.170
				(4.553)*
Adjusted R^2	81.59%	86.67%	87.05%	87.77%

*Significant at the 0.01 level.

Model 1: $R_{jt} = \propto_{0t} + \propto_{1t}\Delta E_{jt}/MV_{jt-1} + \propto_{2t}E_{jt}/MV_{jt-1} + \propto_{3t}\Delta CF_{jt}/MV_{jt-1}$
$+ \propto_{4t}CF_{jt}/MV_{jt-1} + E_{jt}$

Model 2: $R_{jt} = \propto_{0t} + \propto_{1t}\Delta E_{jt}/MV_{jt-1} + \propto_{2t}E_{jt}/MV_{jt-1} + \propto_{3t}\Delta CF_{jt}/MV_{jt-1}$
$+ \propto_{4t}CF_{jt}/MV_{jt-1} + \propto_{5t}MULT_{jt} + E_{2jt}$

Model 3: $R_{jt} = \propto_{0t} + \propto_{1t}\Delta E_{jt}/MV_{jt-1} + \propto_{2t}E_{jt}/MV_{jt-1} + \propto_{3t}\Delta CF_{jt}/MV_{jt-1}$
$+ \propto_{4t}CF_{jt}/MV_{jt-1} + \propto_{5t}MULT_{jt} + \propto_{6t}CR_{jt} + E_{3jt}$

Model 4: $R_{jt} = \propto_{0t} + \propto_{1t}\Delta E_{jt}/MV_{jt-1} + \propto_{2t}E_{jt}/MV_{jt-1} + \propto_{3t}\Delta CF_{jt}/MV_{jt-1}$
$+ \propto_{4t}CF_{jt}/MV_{jt-1} + \propto_{5t}MULT_{jt} + \propto_{6t}CR_{jt} + \propto_{7t}ION_t + \propto_{8t}INF_t + I_{gt}GNP_t + E_{4jt}$

Variable Definitions

R_{jt} = Change in the market value for firm j in year t
MV_{jt} = Market value of firm j at the end of year t
E_{jt} = Earnings for firm j in year t
CF_{jt} = Cash flows from operations for firm j in year t
ΔE_{jt} = Changes in earnings for firm j in year t
ΔCF_{jt} = Changes in cash flows for firm j in year t
$MULT_{jt}$ = Level of multinationality of firm j in year t
CR_{jt} = Corporate reputation score for firm j in year t
ION_t = Index of business formation for year t
INF_t = Annual change in the Consumers' Price Index for year t
GNP_t = Annual change in real GNP for year t

information. As expected and supported in other studies, the evidence suggests that cash flows from operations disclosures required by SFAS No. 95 are consistent with the fundamental information set used by the market in selling security prices. The evidence also suggests that the same fundamental information set includes the nonaccounting variables of multinationality and corporate reputation. This implies, as argued in this study, that investors may view factors such as multinationality and corporate reputation as representing an unbooked or hidden asset, and they value them in the same way as those assets on the firm's balance sheet. The data on multinationality and corporate reputation are made available to the market by both *Forbes* and *Fortune* magazine at a cost equal to the price of an issue of these magazines. They are part of a public disclosure system that eliminates for firms such considerations as costs of developing and presenting disclosures, potential competitive disadvantages, and a host of other factors.

NOTES

1. R. Elliott and P. Jacobson, "Costs and Benefits of Business Information Disclosure," *Accounting Horizons* 6 (December 1994): 80–96.

2. Financial Accounting Standards Board (FASB), *Statement of Cash Flows*, Statement of Financial Accounting Standards No. 95 (Stamford, CT: FASB, 1987).

3. Agnes Cheng, K. H. Chan, and W. Liau, "An Investigation of Market Response to Earnings Announcement: Multinational versus Domestic Firms," *International Journal of Accounting* 32 (1997): 125–138.

4. V. Bernard, "Cross-Sectional Dependence and Problems in Inference in Market-Based Accounting Research," *Journal of Accounting Research* (Spring 1987): 1–48.

5. V. Bernard, "Capital Markets Research in Accounting During the 1980s: A Critical Review." In *The State of Accounting Research as We Enter the 1990s* (University of Illinois Golden Jubilee Symposium, 1989): 72–120.

6. B. Lev, "On the Usefulness of Earnings and Earnings Research: Lessons and Directions from Two Decades of Empirical Research," *Journal of Accounting Research* Supplement (1989): 153–192.

7. Financial Accounting Standards Board (FASB), *Statement of Cash Flows*.

8. A. Ali, "The Incremental Information Content of Earnings, Working Capital from Operations and Cash Flows," *Journal of Accounting Research* (Spring 1994): 61–74.

9. A. Ali and P. Zarowin, "The Role of Earnings Level in Annual Earnings-Return Studies," *Journal of Accounting Research* (Autumn 1992): 286–296.

10. R. Bowen, D. Burgstahler, and L. Daley, "The Incremental Information Content of Accrual versus Cash Flows," *The Accounting Review* (October 1987): 723–747.

11. C. S. Cheng, C. Liu, and T. Schaefer, "Earnings Permanence and the Incremental Information Content of Cash Flows from Operations," *Journal of Accounting Research* (Spring 1996): 173–181.

12. J. Livnat and P. Zarowin, "The Incremental Information Content of Cash-Flow Components," *Journal of Accounting and Economics* (May 1990): 25–46.

13. J. Neil, T. Schaefer, P. Bahnson, and M. Bradbury, "The Usefulness of Cash Flow Data: A Review and Synthesis," *Journal of Accounting Literature* 10 (1991): 117–150.

14. G. Wilson, "The Incremental Information Content of the Accrual and Funds Components of Earnings after Controlling for Earnings," *The Accounting Review* (April 1987): 293–322.

15. Cheng, Chan, and Liau, "An Investigation of Market Response to Earnings Announcement: Multinational Versus Domestic Firms," 125–138.

16. Ali and Zarowin, "The Role of Earnings Level in Annual Earnings-Return Studies," 286–296.

17. Cheng, Chan, and Liau, "An Investigation of Market Response to Earnings Announcement: Multinational Versus Domestic Firms," 125–138.

18. L. Brown, P. Griffin, R. Hagerman, and M. Zmijewski, "An Evaluation of Alternative Proxies for the Market's Assessment of Unexpected Earnings," *Journal of Accounting and Economics* 2 (July 1987): 159–194.

19. Ali and Zarowin, "The Role of Earnings Level in Annual Earnings-Return Studies," 286–296.

20. Cheng, Chan, and Liau, "An Investigation of Market Response to Earnings Announcement: Multinational Versus Domestic Firms," 125–138.

21. George P. Tsetsekos, "Multinationality and Common Stock Offering," *Journal of International Financial Management and Accounting* 3 (1991): 1–16.

22. C. Baldwin, "The Capital Factor: Competing for Capital in Global Environment." In M. Porter, ed. *Competition in Global Industries* (Boston: Harvard Business School Press, 1986): 184–223.

23. B. Kogut, "Foreign Direct Investment as a Sequential Process." In C. P. Kindelberger and D. B. Audretsch, eds. *The Multinational Corporation in the 1980s* (Cambridge, MA: MIT Press, 1993): 38–56.

24. F. Giavazzi and A. Giovannini, *Limiting Exchange Rate Flexibility: The European Monetary System* (Cambridge, MA: MIT Press, 1989).

25. D. Eiteman and A. Stonehill, *Multinational Business Finance* (Boston: Addison-Wesley, 1986).

26. A. Shapiro, *Multinational Financial Management*, 3d ed. (Boston: Allyn & Bacon, 1989).

27. T. Agmon and D. Lessard, "Investor Recognition of Corporate International Diversification," *Journal of Finance* (1977): 1049–1055.

28. V. Errunza and L. Senbert, "The Effects of International Corporate Diversification, Market Valuation and Size Adjusted Evidence," *Journal of Finance* 11 (1981): 717–743.

29. H. Yang, J. Wansley, and W. Lane, "Stock Market Recognition of Multinationality of a Firm and International Events," *Journal of Business Finance and Accounting* 12 (1985): 263–274.

30. Cheng, Chan, and Liau, "An Investigation of Market Response to Earnings Announcement: Multinational Versus Domestic Firms," 125–138.

31. G. R. Dowling, "Managing Your Corporate Images," *Industrial Marketing Management* 15 (1986): 109–115.

32. R. E. Caves and M. E. Porter, "From Entry Barriers to Nobility Barriers," *Quarterly Journal of Economics* 91 (1977): 421–434.

33. B. Klein and K. Leffler, "The Role of Market Forces in Assuring Contractual Performance," *Journal of Political Economy* 85 (1981): 615–641.

34. R. P. Beatty and J. R. Ritter, "Investment Banking, Reputation, and Underpricing of Initial Public Offerings," *Journal of Financial Economics* 15 (1986): 213–232.

35. A. M. Spence, *Market Signaling: Information Transfer in Hiring and Related Screening Process* (Cambridge, MA: Harvard University Press, 1974).

36. C. Fombrum and M. Shanley, "What's in a Name? Reputational Building and Corporate Strategy," *Academy of Management Journal* 33 (1990): 233–258.

37. Ahmed Belkaoui, "Organizational Effectiveness, Social Performance and Economic Performance," *Research in Corporate Social Performance and Policy* 12 (1992): 143–155.

38. Ahmed Riahi-Belkaoui and E. Pavlik, "Asset Management Performance and Reputation Building for Large U.S. Firms," *British Journal of Management* 2 (1991): 231–238.

39. Fombrum and Shanley, "What's in a Name? Reputational Building and Corporate Strategy," 233–258.

40. B. Lev and S. Ramu Thiagarajan, "Fundamental Information Analysis," *Journal of Accounting Research* (Autumn 1993): 190–215.

41. A. Riahi-Belkaoui, "Value Relevance of Popular Ratios," *Advances in Quantitative Analysis of Finance and Accounting* (1997): 193–201.

42. P. Wilson, "The Relative Information Content of Accruals and Cash Flows: Combined Evidence at the Earnings Announcement and Annual Report Release Date," *Journal of Accounting Research* Supplement (1986): 165–200.

43. V. Bernard and T. Stober, "The Nature and Amount of Information in Cash Flows and Accruals," *The Accounting Review* (October 1989): 624–652.

44. *Economic Report of the President* (Washington, DC: U.S. Government Printing Office, 1995).

45. John H. Dunning, "Reappraising the Electric Paradigm in an Age of Alliance Capitalism," *Journal of International Business Studies* 26 (1995): 461–492.

46. John M. Stopford and Louis T. Wells, *Managing the Multinational Enterprise* (New York: Basic Books, 1972).

47. Howard V. Perlmutter, "The Tortuous Evaluation of the Multinational Corporation," *Columbia Journal of World Business* 4 (January-February 1969): 9–18.

48. D. Sullivan, "Measuring the Degree of Internationalization of a Firm," *Journal of International Business Studies* 25 (1994): 325–342.

49. Cheng, Chan, and Liau, "An Investigation of Market Response to Earnings Announcement: Multinational Versus Domestic Firms," 125–138.

50. J. Livnat and P. Zarowin, "The Incremental Information Content of Cash-Flow Components," *Journal of Accounting and Economics* (May 1990): 25–46.

51. D. Belsley, E. Kuh, and R. Welsch, *Regression Diagnostics: Identifying Influential Data and Sources of Collinearity* (New York: Wiley, 1980).

52. H. A. White, "Heteroskedasticity-Consistent Covariance Matrix Estimator and a Direct Test for Heteroskedasticity," *Econometrika* 10 (1980): 817–838.

SELECTED READINGS

Agmon, T., and D. Lessard, "Investor Recognition of Corporate International Diversification." *Journal of Finance* (1977): 1049–1055.

Ali, A. "The Incremental Information Content of Earnings, Working Capital from Operations and Cash Flows." *Journal of Accounting Research* (Spring 1994): 61–74.

Ali, A., and P. Zarowin. "The Role of Earnings Level in Annual Earnings-Return Studies." *Journal of Accounting Research* (Autumn 1992): 286–296.

Baldwin, C. "The Capital Factor: Competing for Capital in Global Environment." In M. Porter, ed. *Competition in Global Industries.* Boston: Harvard Business School Press, 1986: 184–223.

Beatty, R. P., and J. R. Ritter. "Investment Banking, Reputation, and Underpricing of Initial Public Offerings." *Journal of Financial Economics* 15 (1986): 213–232.

Belkaoui, Ahmed. "Organizational Effectiveness, Social Performance and Economic Performance." *Research in Corporate Social Performance and Policy* 12 (1992): 143–155.

Belsley, D., E. Kuh, and R. Welsch. *Regression Diagnostics: Identifying Influential Data and Sources of Collinearity.* New York: Wiley, 1980.

Bernard, V. "Cross-Sectional Dependence and Problems in Inference in Market-

Based Accounting Research." *Journal of Accounting Research* (Spring 1987): 1–48.

———. "Capital Markets Research in Accounting during the 1980s: A Critical Review." In *The State of Accounting Research as We Enter the 1990s*. University of Illinois Golden Jubilee Symposium, 1989: 72–120.

Bernard, V., and T. Stober. "The Nature and Amount of Information in Cash Flows and Accruals." *The Accounting Review* (October 1989): 624–652.

Bowen, R., D. Burgstahler, and L. Daley. "The Incremental Information Content of Accrual versus Cash Flows." *The Accounting Review* (October 1987): 723–747.

Brown, L., P. Griffin, R. Hagerman, and M. Zmijewski. "An Evaluation of Alternative Proxies for the Market's Assessment of Unexpected Earnings." *Journal of Accounting and Economics* 2 (July 1987): 159–194.

Caves, R. E., and M. E. Porter. "From Entry Barriers to Nobility Barriers." *Quarterly Journal of Economics* 91 (1977): 421–434.

Cheng, Agnes, K. H. Chan, and W. Liau. "An Investigation of Market Response to Earnings Announcement: Multinational versus Domestic Firms." *International Journal of Accounting* 32 (1997): 125–138.

Cheng, C. S., C. Liu, and T. Schaefer. "Earnings Permanence and the Incremental Information Content of Cash Flows from Operations." *Journal of Accounting Research* (Spring 1996): 173–181.

Dowling, G. R. "Managing Your Corporate Images." *Industrial Marketing Management* 15 (1986): 109–115.

Dunning, John H. "Reappraising the Eclectic Paradigm in an Age of Alliance Capitalism." *Journal of International Business Studies* 26 (1995): 461–492.

Economic Report of the President. Washington, DC: U.S. Government Printing Office, 1995.

Eiteman, D., and A. Stonehill. *Multinational Business Finance*. Boston: Addison-Wesley, 1986.

Elliott, R., and P. Jacobson. "Costs and Benefits of Business Information Disclosure." *Accounting Horizons* (December 1994): 80–96.

Errunza, V., and L. Senbert. "The Effects of International Corporate Diversification, Market Valuation and Size Adjusted Evidence." *Journal of Finance* 11 (1981): 717–743.

Financial Accounting Standards Board (FASB). *Statement of Cash Flows*. Statement of Financial Accounting Standards No. 95. Stamford, CT: FASB, 1987.

Fombrum, C., and M. Shanley. "What's in a Name? Reputational Building and Corporate Strategy." *Academy of Management Journal* 33 (1990): 233–258.

Giavazzi, F., and A. Giovannini. *Limiting Exchange Rate Flexibility: The European Monetary System.* Cambridge, MA: MIT Press, 1989.

Klein, B., and K. Leffler. "The Role of Market Forces in Assuring Contractual Performance." *Journal of Political Economy* 85 (1981): 615–641.

Kogut, B. "Foreign Direct Investment as a Sequential Process." In C. P. Kindelberger and D. B. Audretsch, eds. *The Multinational Corporation in the 1980s.* Cambridge, MA: MIT Press 1993: 38–56.

Lev, B. "On the Usefulness of Earnings and Earnings Research: Lessons and Directions from Two Decades of Empirical Research." *Journal of Accounting Research* Supplement (1989): 153–192.

Lev, B., and S. Ramu Thiagarajan. "Fundamental Information Analysis." *Journal of Accounting Research* (Autumn 1993): 190–215.

Livnat, J., and P. Zarowin. "The Incremental Information Content of Cash-Flow Components." *Journal of Accounting and Economics* (May 1990): 25–46.

Neil, J., T. Schaefer, P. Bahnson, and M. Bradbury. "The Usefulness of Cash Flow Data: A Review and Synthesis." *Journal of Accounting Literature* 10 (1991): 117–150.

Perlmutter, Howard V. "The Tortuous Evaluation of the Multinational Corporation." *Columbia Journal of World Business* 4 (January–February 1969): 9–18.

Riahi-Belkaoui, A. "Value Relevance of Popular Ratios." *Advances in Quantitative Analysis of Finance and Accounting* (1997): 193–201.

Riahi-Belkaoui, Ahmed, and E. Pavlik. "Asset Management Performance and Reputation Building for Large U.S. Firms." *British Journal of Management* 2 (1991): 231–238.

Shapiro, A. *Multinational Financial Management*, 3d ed. Boston: Allyn & Bacon, 1989.

Spence, A. M. *Market Signaling: Information Transfer in Hiring and Related Screening Process.* Cambridge, MA: Harvard University Press, 1974.

Stopford, John M., and Louis T. Wells. *Managing the Multinational Enterprise.* New York: Basic Books, 1972.

Sullivan, D. "Measuring the Degree of Internationalization of a Firm." *Journal of International Business Studies* 25 (1994): 325–342.

Tsetsekos, George P. "Multinationality and Common Stock Offering." *Journal of International Financial Management and Accounting* 3 (1991): 1–16.

White, H. A. "Heteroskedasticity-Consistent Covariance Matrix Estimator and a Direct Test for Heteroskedasticity." *Econometrika* 10 (1980): 817–838.

Wilson, G. "The Incremental Information Content of the Accrual and Funds Components of Earnings after Controlling for Earnings." *The Accounting Review* (April 1987): 293–322.

Wilson, P. "The Relative Information Content of Accruals and Cash Flows:

Combined Evidence at the Earnings Announcement and Annual Report Release Date.'' *Journal of Accounting Research* Supplement (1986): 165–200.

Yang, H., J. Wansley, and W. Lane. ''Stock Market Recognition of Multinationality of a Firm and International Events.'' *Journal of Business Finance and Accounting* 12 (1985): 263–274.

5

Contextual Accrual and Cash Flow–Based Valuation Models: Impact of Multinationality and Reputation

INTRODUCTION

This chapter investigates the impact of the contextual factors of multinationality and reputation on accrual and cash flow–based valuation. The nature and amount of information on cash flows and accruals was first examined by Wilson[1] using stock behavior around the release of annual reports. He concluded that the market reacts more favorably the larger (smaller) are the cash flows (current accruals). Bernard and Stober[2] were, however, unable to confirm Wilson's results over a longer period, and according to the state of the economy. This chapter extends the works of Wilson and Bernard and Stober in two ways. The first is to assess the generality and robustness of Wilson's results by using a total market value–based valuation model rather than an excess-return–based model.[3] The results confirm Wilson's results. The second is to examine two contextual models of the implications of cash and accruals. We argue that the preference of cash flows over accruals will arise under conditions of high multinationality and high reputation. Support for the hypotheses was found. In sum, we are able to identify the economic logic underlying how the market assimilates information about cash and accruals under the specific contextual environments of multinationality and corporate reputation.

MARKET VALUATION MODELS

A Simplified Model

A simplified model relates market value of equity at the end of a period to the corresponding accruals and cash flows as follows:

$$MV_{it} = a_0 + a_{1i}A_{it} + a_{2i}CF_{it} + e_{it} \tag{1}$$

where:

MV_{it} = Market value of equity of firm i at the end of year t

A_{it} = Total accruals of firm i at the end of year t

CF_{it} = Cash flows of firm i at the end of year t

All variables are deflated by the total assets at the end of year t

Impact of Multinationality

Investors recognize the enhancement of firm value through internationalization. The evidence shows that investors recognize multinationality given that multinational firms show lower systematic risk and unsystematic risk compared to securities of purely domestic firms.[4–6] To test the incremental association between market value of equity and multinationality, after controlling for accruals and cash flows, Model 1 is adjusted as follows:

$$MV_{it} = a_0 + a_{1i}A_{it} + a_{2i}CF_{it} + a_{3i}MULTY_{it} + e'_{it} \tag{2}$$

where:

$MULTY_{it}$ = Level of multinationality of firm i at the end of year t

Impact of Reputation

To create the right impression or reputation, firms signal their key characteristics to constituents in order to maximize their social status.[7] Basically, corporate audiences were found to construct reputation on the basis of accounting and market information or signals regarding firm performance.[8,9] When reputations become established, they constitute signals that may affect the actions of firms' stakeholders, including their shareholders. Specifically, a good reputation can be construed as a competitive advantage within an industry.[10] This implies that investors take corporate reputation into consideration when determining firm value. To test for the incremental association between the market value equity and reputation after controlling for accruals, cash flows, and multinationality, Model 2 is adjusted as follows:

$$MV_{it} = a_0 + a_{1i}A_{it} + a_{2i}CF_{it} + a_{3i}MULTY_{it} + a_{4i}REP_{it} + e^2{}_{it} \qquad (3)$$

where:

REP_{it} = Corporate reputation score for firm i at the end of year t

RESEARCH METHOD

In this study, incremental associations between market value and cash flow from operations, multinationality, and corporate reputation, after controlling for accruals, are presented as evidence of the relevance of the contextual environment of flow-based valuation models. To describe and assess the significance of these relationships, we use three linear regression approaches (Models 1 to 3) that relate market value of equity to the accounting and nonaccounting variables mentioned earlier.

Data and Sample Selection

The population consists of firms included in both *Forbes*' Most International 100 American manufacturing and service firms and *Fortune*'s surveys of corporate reputation from 1987 to 1990. The security data are collected from the CRSP Return files. The accounting variables are collected from COMPUSTAT. Cash flows from operations are reported under SFAS No. 95 (COMPUSTAT item 308). The derivation of the total accruals, multinationality, and corporate reputation variables is explained later. The final sample included 360 firm-year observations that have all the accounting and nonaccounting variables.

Measuring Total Accruals

Total accruals are calculated for each firm as follows[11]:

$$A_{it} = \frac{-DEP_{it}+(AR_{it}-AR_{it-1})+(\text{INV}_{it}-INV_{it-1})-(AP_{it}-AP_{it-1})-(TP_{it}-TP_{it-1})-DT_{it}}{TA_{it}}$$

where:

DEP_{it} = Depreciation expense and the depletion charge for firm i in year t

AR_{it} = Accounts receivable balance for firm i at the end of year t

INV_{it} = Inventory balance for firm i at the end of year t

AP_{it} = Accounts payable for firm i at the end of year t

TP_{it} = Taxes payable balance for firm i at the end of year t

DT_{it} = Deferred tax expense for firm i in year t

TA_{it} = Total asset balance for firm i at the end of year t

Measuring Multinationality

Previous research has attempted to measure the following attributes of multinationality:

1. *Performance*—in terms of what goes on overseas[12]
2. *Structure*—in terms of how resources are used overseas[13]
3. *Attitude or Conduct*—in terms of what is top management orientation[14]

Sullivan[15] developed nine measures of which five were shown to have a high reliability in the construction of homogeneous measures of nationality: (1) foreign sales as a percentage of total sales (FSTS), (2) foreign assets over total assets (FATA), (3) overseas subsidiaries as a percentage of total subsidiaries (OSTS), (4) top management's international experience (TMIE), and (5) psychic dispersion of international operations (PDIO).

In this study we follow a similar approach by measuring multinationality through three measures: (1) foreign sales/total sales (FSTS), (2) foreign profit/total profits (FPTP), and (3) foreign assets/total assets (FATA). As shown in Exhibit 5.1 one common factor appears in intercorrelations among the three variables, as the first eigenvalue alone exceeds the sum of commonalities. The common factor is significantly and positively correlated with the three measures. As pointed out earlier, these factor scores were used to measure the degree of multinationality of firms in the sample.

Measuring Corporate Reputation

The *Fortune* survey covers every industry group comprising four or more companies. The industry groups are based on categories established by the U.S. Office of Management and Budget (OMB). The survey asked executives, directors, and analysts to rate a company on the following eight key attributes of reputation:

1. Quality of management
2. Quality of products/services offered
3. Innovativeness
4. Value as long-term investment
5. Soundness of financial position
6. Ability to attract/develop/keep talented people
7. Responsibility to the community/environment
8. Wise use of corporate assets

Ratings were on a scale of 0 (poor) to 10 (excellent). The score met the multiple-constituency ecological model view of organizational effectiveness. For purposes of this study, the 1987 to 1990 *Fortune* magazine surveys were used. To obtain a unique configuration, a factor analysis is used to isolate the factor common to the eight measures of reputation. All the observations were subjected to factor analysis and one common factor was found to explain the intercorrelations among the eight individual measures. Exhibit 5.2 reports the results of the common factor analysis. One common factor appears to explain the intercorrelations among the eight variables, as the first eigenvalue alone exceeds the sum of the commonalities. The common factor is significantly and positively

Exhibit 5.1

Selected Statistics Related to a Common Factor Analysis of Three Measures of Multinationality for *Forbes'* The Most International 100 U.S. Firms for the 1987-1990 Period

1. Eigenvalues of the Correlation Matrix:

Eigenvalues	1	2	3
	1.8963	0.9169	0.1868

2. Factor Pattern

FACTOR1

FS/TS	0.93853
FP/TP	0.40913
FA/TA	0.92089

3. Final Communality Estimates: Total = 1.389626

FS/TS	FP/TP	FA/TA
0.8808	0.16738	0.84804

4. Standardized Scoring Coefficients

FACTOR1

FS/TS	0.49494
FP/TP	0.21575
FA/TA	0.48563

5. Descriptive Statistics of the Common Factor Extracted from the Three Measures of Multinationality

Maximum	201.059
Third Quartile	52.231
Median	41.50
First Quartile	30.648
Minimum	5.198
Mean	43.062

Variable Definitions
FS/TS = Foreign sales/total sales
FP/TP = Foreign profits/total profits
FA/TA = Foreign assets/total assets

Exhibit 5.2
Selected Statistics Related to a Common Factor Analysis of Measures of Reputation

1.   Eigenvalues of the Correlation Matrix:

Eigenvalues

1	2	3	4	5	6	7	8
6.7805	0.5562	0.3835	0.1343	0.1808	0.0544	0.0476	0.0331

2.   Factor Pattern

FACTOR1

R_1	0.9537	R_4	0.96506	R_7	0.8080
R_2	0.9184	R_5	0.8987	R_8	0.9484
R_3	0.879	R_6	0.9809		

3.   Final Communality Estimates: Total = 1.389626

R_1	R_2	R_3	R_4	R_5	R_6	R_7	R_8
0.9096	0.8435	0.7737	0.9312	0.8077	0.9621	0.6520	0.8996

4.   Standardized Scoring Coefficients

FACTOR1

R_1	0.1406	R_4	0.1423	R_7	0.1191
R_2	0.1354	R_5	0.1325	R_8	0.1398
R_3	0.1279	R_6	0.1446		

5.   Descriptive Statistics of the Common Factor Extracted from the Three Measures of

Multinationality

Maximum	9.001
Third Quartile	7.274
Median	6.604
First Quartile	6.076
Minimum	3.1548
Mean	6.5926

Variable Definitions
R_1 = Quality of management
R_2 = Quality of products/services
R_3 = Innovativeness
R_4 = Value as long-term investment
R_5 = Soundness of financial position
R_6 = Ability to attract, develop and keep talented people
R_7 = Responsibility to the community and environment
R_8 = Wise use of corporate assets

71

correlated with the eight measures. As pointed out earlier, based on the factor scores, high-reputation firms were chosen from the top 24 percent of the distribution factor scores while low-reputation firms were chosen from the bottom 25 percent of the distribution factor scores.

RESULTS

Panel A of Exhibit 5.3 reports description statistics for the variables used in our tests and panel B shows correlation among variables.

The correlations reported in panel B of Exhibit 5.3 show that all correlations between MV_{it}, A_{it}, CF_{it}, $MULTY_{it}$, and REP_{it} are significant at the 0.01 level. The significant associates among other variables indicate some degree of collinearity among the independent variables in the regression analyses. However, the maximum conditions index in all subsequent regressions with earnings and both cash flow variables is only 4.45. Mild collinearity is diagnosed for maximum condition indices between 5 and 10 and severe collinearity for an index over 30. Thus, collinearity does not seem to influence results.

For each of the multivariate regressions to be reported, we perform additional specification tests, including checks for normality and consideration of various scatter plots. A null hypothesis of normality could not be rejected at the 0.01 level in all cases, and the plots revealed some heteroscedasticity but no other obvious problems. Therefore, we calculated the t-statistics after correcting for heteroscedasticity in the manner described by White.

Exhibit 5.4 presents the regression results for Models 1 to 3. Model 1 relates the total market value deflated by total assets to the accruals and cash flows from operations, also deflated by total assets. As shown in Exhibit 5.4, the coefficient for total accruals is significantly negative while the coefficient for cash flows is significantly positive. As expected, the total market value is negatively related to the total accruals and positively related to cash flows. As in Wilson,[16] these results show that the market reacts favorably the larger (smaller) the cash flows (current accruals). At the same time, the results show that accruals and cash flows from operations each provide incremental value-relevance beyond one another in explaining market value.

Model 2 relates the total market value to multinationality in addition to accruals and cash flows from operations. As shown in Exhibit 5.4, the coefficient of multinationality is significantly positive at a 0.01 level. In addition, R^2 increased from 62.96 percent in Model 1 to 73.28 percent

Exhibit 5.3
Descriptive Statistics and Correlations

Panel A: Descriptive Statistics

Variables	Mean	Standard Deviation	Minimum	25%	Median	75%	Maximum
MV_{it}	0.894	0.791	0.018	0.381	0.665	1.132	5
A_t	0.047	0.024	0.010	0.031	0.047	0.062	0.175
CF_i	0.104	0.062	0.052	0.065	0.112	0.143	0.254
$MULTY_{it}$	43.062	19.682	5.198	30.648	41.503	52.231	201.059
REP_{it}	6.592	0.974	3.154	6.076	6.604	7.264	9.001

Panel B: Correlations

	MV_{it}	A_t	CF_i	$MULTY_{it}$	REP_{it}
MV_{it}	1.000				
A_t	0.061*	1.000			
CF_i	0.717*	0.454*	1.000		
$MULTY_{it}$	0.096*	0.023	-0.012	1.000	
REP_{it}	0.512*	0.070	0.495*	0.009	1.000

*Significant at the 0.01 level.

Variable Definitions

MV_{it} = Market value of equity for firm i in period t
A_{it} = Total accruals for firm i in period t
CF_{it} = Cash flows from operations for firm i in period t
$MULTY_{it}$ = Index of multinationality for firm i in period t
REP_{it} = Index of complete reputation for firm i in period t

Exhibit 5.4
Regression Results of Linear Models[1]

	Model 1	Model 2	Model 3
Intercept	0.17035	-0.1082	-0.6129
	(2.737)*	(-1.36)	(-2.870)*
A_{it}	-11.2791	-16.7071	-16.2253
	(-9.521)*	(-14.621)*	(-12.406)*
CF_{it}	11.8366	14.6982	13.8484
	(24.703)*	(30.106)*	(22.240)*
$MULTY_{it}$		0.0043	0.0047
		(3.3347)*	(3.253)
REP_{it}			0.0821
			(2.534)*
Adjusted R^2	0.6296	0.7328	0.7588
n	360		

[1]Model 1: $MV_{it} = a_0 + a_{1i}A_{it} + a_{2i}CF_{it} + e_{it}$
Model 2: $MV_{it} = a_0 + a_{1i}A_{it} + a_{2i}CF_{it} + a_{3i}MULTY_{it} + e^1_{it}$
Model 3: $MV_{it} = a_0 + a_{1i}A_{it} + a_{2i}CF_{it} + a_{3i}MULTY_{it} + a_{4i}REP_{it} + e^2_{it}$
[2]MV_{it} = Market value of equity of firm i at the end of year t
A_{it} = Total accruals of firm i at the end of year t
CF_{it} = Cash flows of firm i at the end of year t
$MULTY_{it}$ = Level of multinationality of firm i at the end of year t
REP_{it} = Corporate reputation score for firm i at the end of year t
*Significant at the 0.01 level.

in Model 2. The evidence suggests that multinationality provides incremental value-relevance beyond accruals and cash flows in explaining market value.

Model 3 relates the market value to the accounting variables of accruals and cash flows and the nonaccounting variables of multinationality and corporate reputation. As shown in Exhibit 5.4, the coefficient for corporate reputation (0.0821) is significantly positive at the 0.01 level. This evidence suggests that corporate reputation provides incremental value-relevance beyond accruals, cash flows, and multinationality in explaining market value.

SUMMARY AND CONCLUSIONS

The chapter examined the generality and robustness of an accrual and cash flow–based model that includes the contextual factors of multinationality and corporate reputation. The evidence confirms previous results presented by Wilson[17] using total market value as a dependent variable and a price level rather than a return/changes regression. Basically the market value is larger the larger (smaller) the cash flows (current accruals). In addition, the preference of cash flows over accruals arises under conditions of high multinationality and high corporate reputation. The results verify the economic logic underlying how the market assimilates information about cash and accruals under the specific contexts of multinationality and reputation. First, a price level regression seems to provide a better specification of this economic logic. Second, contextual factors play a fundamental role in the same economic logic. Future research needs to examine the role of other contextual factors in the determination of the relationship between the market value and accruals and cash flows.

NOTES

1. P. Wilson "The Relative Information Content of Accruals and Cash Flows: Combined Evidence at the Earnings Announcement and Annual Report Release Date," *Journal of Accounting Research* (September 1986): 165–200.

2. V. Bernard and T. Stober, "The Nature and Amount of Information in Cash Flows and Accruals," *The Accounting Review* (October 1989): 624–652.

3. Kothari and Zimmerman (1994) argue that in situations where prices lead earnings, price level regressions are better specified than return/changes regressions for estimating the price-earnings relation.

4. T. Agmon and D. Lessard, "Investor Recognition of Corporate International Diversification," *Journal of Finance* (1977): 1049–1055.

5. V. Errunza and L. Senbert, "The Effects of International Corporate Diversification, Market Valuation and Size Adjusted Evidence," *Journal of Finance* 11 (1981): 717–743.

6. H. Yang, J. Wansley, and W. Lane, "Stock Market Recognition of Multinationality of a Firm and International Events," *Journal of Business, Finance, and Accounting* 12 (1985): 263–274.

7. A. M. Spence, *Market Signaling: Information Transfer in Hiring and Related Screening Process* (Cambridge, MA: Harvard University Press, 1974).

8. C. Fombrum and M. Shanley, "What's in a Name? Reputational Building and Corporate Strategy," *Academy of Management Journal* 33 (1990): 233–258.

9. Ahmed Riahi-Belkaoui and E. Pavlik, "Asset Management Performance and Reputation Building for Large U.S. Firms," *British Journal of Management* 2 (1991): 231–238.

10. Fombrum and Shanley, "What's in a Name? Reputational Building and Corporate Strategy," 233–258.

11. P. M. Healy, "The Effect of Bonus Schemes on Accounting Decisions," *Journal of Accounting and Economics* 7 (1985): 85–107.

12. John H. Dunning, "Reappraising the Eclectic Paradigm in an Age of Alliance Capitalism," *Journal of International Business Studies* 26 (1995): 461–492.

13. John M. Stopford and Louis T. Wells, *Managing the Multinational Enterprise* (New York: Basic Books, 1972).

14. H. V. Perlmutter, "The Tortuous Evaluation of the Multinational Corporation," *Columbia Journal of World Business* 4 (1969): 9–18.

15. Daniel Sullivan, "Measuring the Degree of Internationalization of a Firm," *Journal of International Business Studies* 25 (1994): 325–342.

16. Wilson, "The Relative Information Content of Accruals and Cash Flows: Combined Evidence at the Earnings Announcement and Annual Report Release Date," 165–200.

17. Ibid.

SELECTED READINGS

Agmon, T., and D. Lessard. "Investor Recognition of Corporate International Diversification." *Journal of Finance* (1977): 1049–1055.

Belkaoui, Ahmed. "Organizational Effectiveness, Social Performance and Economic Performance." *Research in Corporate Social Performance and Policy* 12 (1992): 143–155.

Bernard, V., and T. Stober. "The Nature and Amount of Information in Cash Flows and Accruals." *The Accounting Review* (October 1989): 624–652.

Dunning, John H. "Reappraising the Eclectic Paradigm in an Age of Alliance Capitalism." *Journal of International Business Studies* 26 (1995): 461–492.

Errunza, V., and L. Senbert. "The Effects of International Corporate Diversification, Market Valuation and Size Adjusted Evidence." *Journal of Finance* 11 (1981): 717–743.

Fombrum, C., and M. Shanley. "What's in a Name? Reputational Building and Corporate Strategy." *Academy of Management Journal* 33 (1990): 233–258.

Helay, P. M. "The Effect of Bonus Schemes on Accounting Decisions." *Journal of Accounting and Economics* 7 (1985): 85–107.

Perlmutter, H. V. "The Tortuous Evaluation of the Multinational Corporation." *Columbia Journal of World Business* 4 (1969): 9–18.

Riahi-Belkaoui, Ahmed, and E. Pavlik. "Asset Management Performance and Reputation Building for Large U.S. Firms." *British Journal of Management* 2 (1991): 231–238.

Spence, A. M. *Market Signaling: Information Transfer in Hiring and Related Screening Process.* Cambridge, MA: Harvard University Press, 1974.

Stopford, John M., and Louis T. Wells. *Managing the Multinational Enterprise*. New York: Basic Books, 1972.

Sullivan, Daniel. "Measuring the Degree of Internationalization of a Firm." *Journal of International Business Studies* 25 (1994): 325–342.

Wilson, P. "The Relative Information Content of Accruals and Cash Flows: Combined Evidence at the Earnings Announcement and Annual Report Release Date." *Journal of Accounting Research* (September 1986): 165–200.

Yang, H., J. Wansley, and W. Lane. "Stock Market Recognition of Multinationality of a Firm and International Events." *Journal of Business, Finance, and Accounting* 12 (1985): 263–274.

6

Multinationality and Earnings Management

INTRODUCTION

This chapter develops and tests the hypothesis that managers of high-multinationality firms make accounting choices to reduce reported earnings compared to managers of low-multinationality firms. Unlike other studies, we assume that earnings management is a present and continuous phenomenon rather than a behavior conditioned by an eventual crisis. While all firms are potentially resorting to earnings management, the level of multinationality is assumed to affect the nature of earnings management with high-multinationality firms potentially resorting to income-reducing accruals. We argue that high levels of multinationality cause higher profitability and higher reported accounting numbers. A result of the higher reported accounting numbers is the possible perception of the accounting rates of return as ''excessive'' and indicative of monopolistic power on the part of the firm, thereby increasing both the political costs and the political risk. In such a case, managers' reporting of lower earnings may be expected to reduce both political costs and political risk.

Accrual analysis, similar to that of Jones,[1] Cahan,[2] and Hall and Stammerjohan,[3] is performed on a sample of high-and low-multinationality firms to determine the extent of earnings management. Our findings indicate that managers of high-multinationality firms facing potentially high political costs and political risk report income-decreasing accruals compared to low-multinationality firms.

The remainder of the study is organized as follows. The next section develops the relationship between multinationality and earnings management, followed by a description of the research design. A description of the sample selection and research method is included in the next section. Results are presented next, followed by a summary and conclusion.

MULTINATIONALITY AND EARNINGS MANAGEMENT

The multinational firm is a collection of valuable options and generates profits that enhance its value.[4] The arbitrage benefits result from (a) the exploitation of various institutional imperfections; (b) timing options; (c) technology options; and (d) staging options.[5,6] Better financing bargains,[7] as well as capital availability,[8,9] are also possible through internationalization. In addition, multinational firms can achieve arbitrage benefits in financing cash flows by (a) exploiting financial bargains; (b) reducing taxes on financial flows; and (c) mitigating risks by shifting them to agents with a comparative advantage in beating them.[10,11] These arbitrage benefits have resulted in both higher profitability[12,13] and higher political risk.[14] Both increased profitability and political risk are expected to induce managers to resort to income-reducing accruals.

First, the increase in the profitability of multinational firms increases both their political visibility and political costs. The political-cost hypothesis predicts that managers confronted with the possibility of politically imposed wealth transfer will resort to earnings management to reduce the likelihood and size of this transfer.[15] Thus, high-multinationality and high-income firms that are particularly vulnerable to wealth-extracting political transfers in the form of legislation and/or regulation will have an incentive to resort to accruals to reduce their reported income numbers compared to low-multinationality and low-income firms.

Second, political risk is a phenomenon that characterizes an unfriendly climate to visibly profitable multinational firms.[16] It refers to the potential economic losses arising as a result of governmental measures or special situations that may limit or prohibit the multinational activities of a firm. One way to limit the potential emergence of political risk is to reduce the reported earnings number. Earnings management in high-multinational firms may be a way of reducing the factors mitigating the emergence of political risk.

We hypothesize that high-multinational firms make accounting choices to reduce income and net worth compared to low-multinationality firms.

H1: High-multinationality firms make income-decreasing accruals compared to low-multinationality firms.

RESEARCH DESIGN

The objective of the design is to examine the potential relationships between multinationality and the total accruals of firms as those accruals reflect accounting choices made by management. The technique used by Jones[17] and Cahan[18] for the estimation of nondiscretionary accruals is adopted in this study. It estimates nondiscretionary accruals by regressing total accruals on the change in sales (a proxy for level of activity) and on the fixed-asset balance. The approach leads to an estimate of discretionary accruals that is less biased and less noisy than earlier models and eliminates the assumption that accruals remain stationary over time. The basic model is as follows:

$$A_{it} = b_0 + b_1 CHSALES_{it} + b_2 FIXASSETS_{it} + e_{it} \tag{1}$$

where:

$$A_{it} = \text{Total accruals in year } t/\text{Total Assets}_{it}$$
$$CHSALES_{it} = \text{Change in sales from year } t - 1 \text{ to year } t$$
$$(\text{Sales Revenue}_{it} - \text{Sales Revenue }_{it-1})/\text{Total Assets}_{it}$$
$$FIXASSETS_{it} = \text{Fixed assets at the end of year } t \text{ (Fixed Assets}_{it})/\text{Total Assets}_{it}$$

In the estimation process, Model 1 is expanded to include an indicator variable to measure the discretionary accruals of high-multinationality firms. The expansion also includes total assets as a measure of size and dummy variables for each year of analysis.

The effect of multinationality is tested by estimating Model 3.

$$A_{it} = b_0 + b_1 CHSALES_{it} + b_2 FIXASSETS_{it} + b_3 MULTY_{it}$$
$$+ b_4 TA_{it} + b_5 YR_{it} \cdots + b_9 YR_{it} \tag{2}$$

where TA is total assets and YR is a dummy variable for a year of analysis.

The expected sign of the coefficient for $CHSALES$ is positive. It is expected to be negative for all the other explanatory variables. The coefficient of $MULTY$ will be negative if managers lower accruals for high-multinationality firms.

As in Hall and Stammerjohan,[19] a two-step generalized least-square error components model is used in this study, as it is more efficient than the within-group estimator, fixed-effects covariance model used by Cahan.[20]

DATA

Sample and Method

The sample consisted of all the firms included in *Forbes'* Most International 100 American manufacturing and service firms in the 1987 to 1990 period. Financial data were collected from both the *Forbes* articles and COMPUSTAT. Total accruals are calculated for each firm as follows:

$$A_{it} = \frac{-DEP_{it} + (AR_{it} - AR_{it-1}) + (INV_{it} - INV_{it-1}) - (AP_{it} - AP_{it-1}) - (TP_{it} - TP_{it-1}) - DT_{it}}{TA_{it}} \tag{3}$$

where:

DEP_{it} = Depreciation expense and the depletion charge for firm i in year t

AR_{it} = Accounts receivable balance for firm i at the end of year t

INV_{it} = Inventory balance for firm i at the end of year t

AP_{it} = Accounts payable for firm i at the end of year t

TP_{it} = Taxes payable balance for firm i at the end of year t

DT_{it} = Deferred tax expense for firm i in year t

TA_{it} = Total asset balance for firm i at the end of year t

The data are pooled over time and across firms, resulting in a sample of 339 firm-years. To test the effect of multinationality on discretionary accruals, a dichotomous indicator variable, *MULTY*, is added to Model 1. *MULTY* takes on the value of one for the group of firms classified as high-multinationality firms and zero for firms classified as low-multinationality firms. Model 1 is also expanded to include YR_{it}, dummy-coded variable as 1 for year t ($t = 1987–1990$), and TA_{it} for the total assets of the firm. The *YR* variables measure the time effect for each of the four years. The *TA* variable is added as a result of the size hypothesis whereby large firms are expected to make income-decreasing choices relative to small firms.[21] The effect of size is important given the evidence presented later about the significant difference in size between the high-multinationality and the low-multinationality firms.

Measuring Multinationality

Previous research has attempted to measure three attributes of the degree of multinationality:

1. *Performance*—in terms of what goes on overseas[22]
2. *Structure*—in terms of how resources are used overseas[23]
3. *Attitude or Conduct*—in terms of what is top management orientation[24]

Nine measures were identified to include: (1) foreign sales as a percentage of total sales (FSTS), (2) research and development intensity (RDI), (3) advertising intensity (AI), (4) export sales as a percentage of total sales (ESTS), (5) foreign profits as a percentage of total profits (FPTP), (6) foreign assets over total assets (FATA), (7) overseas subsidiaries as a percentage of total subsidiaries (OSTS), (8) top management's international experience (TMIE), and (9) psychic dispersion of international operations (PDIO).[25] Of these nine measures, an item-total analysis showed the five variables of FSTS, FATA, OSTS, PDIO, and TMIE to have reliability in the construction of a homogeneous measure of multinationality.[26] We follow a similar approach in this study, using an ensemble of variables to measure multinationality. Three measures of multinationality generally available are used in this study: foreign sales/total assets (FSTS), foreign profits/total profits (FPTP), and foreign assets/total assets (FATA). To obtain a unique contribution, a factor analysis is used to isolate the factor common to the three measures of multinationality. All the observations were subjected to factor analysis and one common factor was found to explain the intercorrelations among the three individual measures. Exhibit 6.1 reports the results of the common factor analysis. One factor appears to explain the intercorrelations among the three variables, as the first eigenvalue alone exceeds the sum of commonalities. The common factor is significantly and positively correlated with the three measures. As pointed out earlier, based on these factor scores, high-multinationality firms were chosen from the top 25 percent of the distribution factor scores while low-multinationality firms were chosen from the bottom 25 percent of the distribution factor scores. Descriptive statistics for selected variables and the factor scores are presented in Exhibit 6.2.

TESTS AND RESULTS

The results for the error-components estimation of Model 1 are reported in Exhibit 6.3. As expected, both *CHSALES* and *FIXASSETS* are statistically significant. The overall model is also significant with an *F*-value of 32.618 and an adjusted R^2 of 15 percent. It appears that a significant portion of the variation in accruals of multinational firms can be explained by changes in sales and the fixed-asset balance.

The error-components regression results for Model 2 are reported in Exhibit 6.4. The results support the view that the variation in accruals can be explained by the change in sales, the fixed-asset balance, and time-dependent effects. In addition, the variable of interest, *MULTY*, is significant at the 0.04 level, with a one-tailed test, and its sign is negative. Because high multinationality was coded as 1, the negative sign of *MULTY* indicates that discretionary accruals of high-multinationality firms were lower than low-multinationality firms, which supports the political cost and political risk hypotheses.

SUMMARY AND CONCLUSIONS

This study examines, on a longitudinal basis, whether managers of multinational firms respond to the political costs associated with a high level of multinationality by adjusting their discretionary accruals. The discretionary accruals for the 100 largest U.S. multinationals were examined over the 1987–1990 period by using the residuals of a fixed-effects covariance model that regressed total accruals on the change in

Exhibit 6.1

Selected Statistics Related to a Common Factor Analysis of Three Measures of Multinationality for *Forbes'* The Most International 100 U.S. Firms for the 1987-1990 Period

1. Eigenvalues of the Correlation Matrix:

Eigenvalues	1	2	3
	1.8963	0.9169	0.1868

2. Factor Pattern

   FACTOR1

FS/TS	0.93853
FP/TP	0.40913
FA/TA	0.92089

3. Final Communality Estimates: Total = 1.389626

FS/TS	FP/TP	FA/TA
0.8808	0.16738	0.84804

4. Standardized Scoring Coefficients

   FACTOR1

FS/TS	0.49494
FP/TP	0.21575
FA/TA	0.48563

5. Descriptive Statistics of the Common Factor Extracted from the Three Measures of Multinationality

Maximum	201.059
Third Quartile	52.231
Median	41.50
First Quartile	30.648
Minimum	5.198
Mean	43.062

Variable Definitions
FS/TS = Foreign sales/total sales
FP/TP = Foreign profits/total profits
FA/TA = Foreign assets/total assets

Exhibit 6.2
Descriptive Statistics

A. High-Multinationality Sample

Variables	Mean	Standard Deviation	Maximum	Median	Minimum
Foreign Revenues/ Total Revenues	39.53	1554	75.1	39.85	9.2
Foreign Profit/Total Profit	55.97	39.09	315.9	50.8	10.7
Foreign Assets/ Total Assets	32.33	11.78	58.8	29.5	7.8
Total Revenues (thousands)	3554.8	29002.1	136932	24081	6672
Total Assets (thousands)	53146.3	50198.3	231768	34465	7451
Net Profit (thousands)	1715	1720.01	8020	1305	.4407
Score	47.96	17.27	89.27	44.69	12.00

B. Low-Multinationality Sample

Variables	Mean	Standard Deviation	Maximum	Median	Minimum
Foreign Revenues/ Total Revenues	30.75	11.71	74.9	30.00	9.6
Foreign Profit/Total Profit	39.90	34.13	230	27.30	0.1
Foreign Assets/ Total Assets	28.88	12.84	84.7	27.35	3.6
Total Revenues	6458.09	3093.3	17803	5734	2318
Total Assets	9459.35	14813.01	118250	5154	2034
Net Profit	344.83	320.27	1124.3	352.2	-515.2
Score	38.13	15.82	96.08	36.03	8.82

Exhibit 6.3
Results of Regression Estimation—Model 1
$A_{it} = b_0 + b_1 CHSALES_{it} + b_2 FIXASSETS_{it} + e_{it}$

Interdependent Variables	Expected Sign	Coefficient	t-value	One-tailed probability
Intercept		-0.0236	7.328	0.0001
CHSALES	+	0.0160	4.049	0.0001
FIXASSETS	−	-0.1431	-7.675	0.0001
n=	339			
R²		0.1622	F statistics	Probability
Adjusted R²		0.1572	32.618	0.0001

Variable Definitions

$$A_{it} = (AR_{it} - AR_{it-1} + INV_{it} - INV_{it-1} - AP_{it} + AP_{it-1} - TP_{it} + TP_{it-1} - DEP_{it} - DT_{it})/TA_{it}$$

where:

DEP	=	depreciation expense
AR	=	accounts receivable
INV	=	inventory
AP	=	accounts payable
TP	=	taxes payable
DT	=	deferred tax expense
TA	=	total assets
$CHSALES_{it}$	=	(net $sales_{it}$ − net $sales_{it-1}$)/TA_{it}
$FIXASSETS_{it}$	=	fixed $assets_{it}$/TA_{it}

sales, the fixed-asset balance, and a dummy variable for each year of study. The hypothesis is tested using a tested design with a dummy variable, coded one for high multinationality, included in the accrual model. This multinationality variable was significant and negatively signed, which indicates that the discretionary accruals were lower for high-multinationality firms. The results support the political cost and political risk hypotheses associated with multinationality and are consistent with the view that managers adjust earnings in response to a high level of multinationality.

The results, however, are limited because the sample includes only the largest U.S. multinationals. This limitation suggests one area for future research. The longitudinal approach could be extended to explore responses to a wider range of multinationality.

Exhibit 6.4

Results of Regression Estimation—Model 2

$A_{it} = b_0 + b_1 CHSALES_{it} + b_2 FIXASSETS_{it} + b_3 MULTY_{it} + b_4 TA_{it}$
$+ b_5 YR_{it} + b_6 YR_{i2} + b_7 YR_{i3}$

Interdependent Variables	Expected Sign	Coefficient	t-value	One-tailed probabality
Intercept		-0.0146	-2.470	0.0146
CHSALES	+	0.0026	4.155	0.0002
FIXASSETS	+	-0.1717	-6.436	0.0001
MULTY	−	-0.0080	-2.555	0.0116
TA	−	-0.0000006	-2.487	0.0102
YR_1		-0.0029	-4.758	0.0001
YR_2		-0.0018	-4.051	0.0001
YR_3		-0.00122	-4.330	0.0001
R^2		0.3411	F statistics	Probability
Adjusted R^2		0.3121	4.758	0.0001
n	166			

Variable Definitions

TA   = Total assets
YR   = Year
MULTY = 1 if multinationality is high, 0 if multinationality is low

NOTES

1. J. Jones, "Earnings Management during Import Relief Investigations," *Journal of Accounting Research* 29 (Autumn 1991): 193–228.

2. S. Cahan, "The Effect of Antitrust Investigations on Discretionary Accruals: A Refined Test of the Political-Cost Hypothesis," *The Accounting Review* 67 (January 1992): 77–95.

3. S. C. Hall and W. W. Stammerjohan, "Damage Awards and Earnings Management in the Oil Industry," *The Accounting Review* 1 (January 1997): 47–65.

4. George P. Tsetsekos, "Multinationality and Common Stock Offering," *Journal of International Financial Management and Accounting* 3 (1991): 1–16.

5. John Dunning, "Reappraising the Eclectic Paradigm in an Age of Alliance Capitalism," *Journal of International Business Studies* 26 (1995): 461–492.

6. Bruce Kogut, "Designing Global Strategies: Profiting from Operational Flexibility," *Sloan Management Review* (1991): 27–38.

7. F. Giavazzi and A. Giovannini, *Limiting Exchange Rate Flexibility: The European Monetary System* (Cambridge, MA: MIT Press, 1989).

8. D. Eiteman and A. Stonehill, *Multinational Business Finance* (Boston: Addison-Wesley, 1986).

9. A. Riahi-Belkaoui, *International and Multinational Accounting* (London: Dryden Press, 1994).

10. Tsetsekos, "Multinationality and Common Stock Offering," 1–16.

11. A. Riahi-Belkaoui, "Multinationality and Corporate Financing Policies," *Advances in Financial Planning and Forecasting* 7 (1997): 207–215.

12. Daniel Sullivan, "Measuring the Degree of Internationalization of a Firm," *Journal of International Business Studies* 25 (1994): 325–342.

13. A. Riahi-Belkaoui, *Multinationality and Financial Performance* (Westport, CT: Greenwood Publishing, 1996).

14. J. Monti-Belkaoui and A. Riahi-Belkaoui, *The Nature, Estimation and Management of Political Risk* (Westport, CT: Greenwood Publishing, 1999).

15. R. L. Watts and J. L. Zimmerman, "Towards a Positive Theory of Determination of Accounting Standards," *The Accounting Review* 53 (January 1978): 112–134.

16. Monti-Belkaoui and Riahi-Belkaoui, *The Nature, Estimation and Management of Political Risk.*

17. Jones, "Earnings Management during Import Relief Investigations," 193–228.

18. Cahan, "The Effect of Antitrust Investigations on Discretionary Accruals: A Refined Test of the Political-Cost Hypothesis," 77–95.

19. Hall and Stammerjohan, "Damage Awards and Earnings Management in the Oil Industry," 47–65.

20. Cahan, "The Effect of Antitrust Investigations on Discretionary Accruals: A Refined Test of the Political-Cost Hypothesis," 77–95.

21. A. A. Christie, "Aggregation of Test Statistics: An Evaluation of the Evidence on Contracting and Size Hypotheses," *Journal of Accounting and Economics* 12 (January 1990): 15–36.

22. Dunning, "Reappraising the Eclectic Paradigm in an Age of Alliance Capitalism," 461–492.

23. John M. Stopford and Louis T. Wells, *Managing the Multinational Enterprise* (New York: Basic Books, 1972).

24. H. V. Perlmutter, "The Tortuous Evaluation of the Multinational Corporation," *Columbia Journal of World Business* 4 (1969): 9–18.

25. Sullivan, "Measuring the Degree of Internationalization of a Firm," 325–342.

26. Ibid.

SELECTED READINGS

Cahan, S. "The Effect of Antitrust Investigations on Discretionary Accruals: A Refined Test of the Political-Cost Hypothesis." *The Accounting Review* 67 (January 1992): 77–95.

Christie, A. A. "Aggregation of Test Statistics: An Evaluation of the Evidence on Contracting and Size Hypotheses." *Journal of Accounting and Economics* 12 (January 1990): 15–36.

Dunning, John. "Reappraising the Eclectic Paradigm in an Age of Alliance Capitalism." *Journal of International Business Studies* 26 (1995): 461–492.

Eiteman, D., and A. Stonehill. *Multinational Business Finance*. Boston: Addison-Wesley, 1986.

Giavazzi, F., and A. Giovannini. *Limiting Exchange Rate Flexibility: The European Monetary System*. Cambridge, MA: MIT Press, 1989.

Hall, S. C., and W. W. Stammerjohan. "Damage Awards and Earnings Management in the Oil Industry." *The Accounting Review* 1 (January 1997): 47–65.

Healy, S. C. "Political Scrutiny and Earnings Management in the Oil Refining Industry." *Journal of Accounting and Public Policy* 12 (Winter 1993): 325–351.

Jones, J. "Earnings Management during Import Relief Investigations." *Journal of Accounting Research* 29 (Autumn 1991): 193–228.

Kogut, Bruce. "Designing Global Strategies: Profiting from Operational Flexibility." *Sloan Management Review* (1991): 27–38.

Monti-Belkaoui, J., and A. Riahi-Belkaoui. *The Nature, Estimation and Management of Political Risk*. Westport, CT: Greenwood Publishing, 1999.

Perlmutter, H. V. "The Tortuous Evaluation of the Multinational Corporation." *Columbia Journal of World Business* 4 (1969): 9–18.

Riahi-Belkaoui, A. *International and Multinational Accounting*. London: Dryden Press, 1994.

———. *Multinationality and Financial Performance*. Westport, CT: Greenwood Publishing, 1996.

———. "Multinationality and Corporate Financing Policies." *Advances in Financial Planning and Forecasting* 7 (1997): 207–215.

Stopford, John M., and Louis T. Wells. *Managing the Multinational Enterprise*. New York: Basic Books, 1972.

Sullivan, Daniel. "Measuring the Degree of Internationalization of a Firm." *Journal of International Business Studies* 25 (1994): 325–342.

Tsetsekos, George P. "Multinationality and Common Stock Offering." *Journal of International Financial Management and Accounting* 3 (1991): 1–16.

Watts, R. L., and J. L. Zimmerman. "Towards a Positive Theory of Determination of Accounting Standards." *The Accounting Review* 53 (January 1978): 112–134.

7

The Association between Systematic Risk and Multinationality: A Growth Opportunities Perspective

INTRODUCTION

The multinationality of a firm is the degree of its international diversification and involvement. The question is whether a firm can truly reduce its systematic risk (measured by the market model beta) by increasing its multinationality. Various studies have examined the issue of the association between level of multinationality and systematic risk. The overwhelming evidence is of a negative relationship between systematic risk and multinationality.[1-5] With one exception[6] these studies did not control for accounting variables found to be able to explain and forecast market risk.[7-10] In addition, all these studies failed to investigate the impact of growth opportunities, as measured by the investment opportunity set, on the relationships between systematic risk and multinationality. This study corrects for both limitations by (1) investigating the association between multinationality and systematic risk after controlling for corporate reputation and other factors known to be associated with systematic risk and (2) evaluating the impact of the investment opportunity set on the association. Briefly, the results of this study suggest that (1) systematic risk is positively related to multinationality even after controlling for corporate reputation and other known factors, and (2) the relation is, however, negative for high-investment opportunity set firms and only positive for low-investment opportunity set firms.

The second section of this chapter discusses the development of hypotheses. The next section discusses the methods and measures. Results are then presented, followed by a concluding section.

DEVELOPMENT OF HYPOTHESES

The benefits of multinationality are essentially in terms of higher returns. However, the multinational stock prices are also affected by foreign and local factors. Therefore, multinationality is most likely to have an effect on the betas of multinational firms. The risk characteristics of the multinational firm most likely reflect the overall firm's characteristics as well as the foreign environment. *Our main hypothesis is of a positive association between the systematic risk of a multinational firm and its level of multinationality.* However, as stated earlier, there is a lot of evidence of a negative relationship between systematic risk and multinationality. This evidence is due to the failure to account for the role of growth opportunities in the relationship between multinationality and systematic risk. The eclectic paradigm of international production specifies ownership advantages as one of the three determinants of the extent, form, and pattern of international production.[11,12] These ownership advantages include both proprietary know-how (unique assets) and transactional advantages that outweigh the costs of servicing an unfamiliar or distant environment. Basically, the multinational firm possesses unique ownership advantages that its competitors do not possess. These unique ownership advantages are the future investment options of the firm or growth opportunities. The firm may be viewed as a combination of assets-in-place and future investment options. The lower the proportion of firm value represented by assets-in-place, the higher the growth opportunities. Myers[13] describes these potential investment opportunities as call options whose values depend on the likelihood that management will exercise them. Like call options, the growth options represent value to the firm.[14] These growth options are intangible assets or ownership advantages that represent the investment opportunity set. The higher these growth options, the more beneficial is multinationality. In other words, in terms of our research question, the higher the growth options, the most likely the association between multinationality and systematic risk will be negative. *Our second hypothesis is of a negative association between the systematic risk and multinationality of a firm with high growth options.*

METHODS

Sample

The population consists of firms included in both *Forbes*' Most International 100 American manufacturing and service firms and *Fortune*'s surveys of corporate reputation from 1987 to 1990. The security data are selected from the CRSP Return files. The accounting variables are collected from both COMPUSTAT and *Forbes* articles. The corporate reputation measures are collected from *Fortune*'s surveys. The derivation of the multinationality and reputation measures indices is explained later. The final sample includes 322 firm-year observations.

Control Variable Selection

Various studies attempted to explain and forecast market risk using accounting variables.[15–19] Three variables consistently identified as related to systematic risk are leverage (positive relationship), size (negative relationship), and earnings variability (positive relationship). Accordingly, these three variables are used in this study as control variables. In addition to these three variables, this study uses corporate reputation as another control variable. To create the right impression or reputation, firms signal their key characteristics to constituents to maximize their social status.[20] Basically, corporate audiences were found to construct reputations on the basis of accounting and market information or signals regarding firm performance.[21–23] These reputations have become established and constitute signals that may affect the actions of firms' stakeholders, including their shareholders.

Method of Analyzing the Effect of Multinationality on Systematic Risk

To analyze the effect of multinationality on systematic risk, we estimate the following regression:

$$BETA_{it} = \alpha_0 + \alpha_1 MULTY_{it} + \alpha_2 REP_{it} + \alpha_3 VROA_{it}$$
$$+ \alpha_4 LEV_{it} + \alpha_5 SIZE_{it} + E_{it} \tag{1}$$

where:

$BETA_{it}$ = Systematic risk of firm i for period t

$MULTY_{it}$ = Multinationality score of firm i for period t

REP_{it} = Reputation score of firm i for period t

$VROA_{it}$ = Variance of return in assets of firm i for period t where the variance is computed over the eight quarters beginning with the first quarter of the year of observation

LEV_{it} = Leverage of firm i for period t, computed as the ratio equity to total assets

$SIZE_{it}$ = Size measure as logarithm of total assets of firm i for period t

The related research, discussed above, suggests that α_2, α_3, α_4, $\alpha_5 > 0$. In the context of equation (1) the first hypothesis is H_1: $\alpha_1 > 0$. Our second hypothesis is H_2: $\alpha_1 < 0$ for high-growth firms. All the analyses are conducted on observations that are pooled cross-sectionally over time.

MEASURES

Measuring Multinationality

Previous research has attempted to measure the following attributes of multinationality:

1. *Performance*—in terms of what goes on overseas[24]
2. *Structure*—in terms of resources used overseas[25]
3. *Attitude or Conduct*—in terms of what is top management's orientation[26]

Sullivan[27] developed nine measures of which five were shown to have a high reliability in the construction of homogeneous measures of nationality: (1) foreign sales as a percentage of total sales (FSTS), (2) foreign assets over total assets (FATA), (3) overseas subsidiaries as a percentage of total subsidiaries (OSTS), (4) top management's international experience (TMIE), and (5) psychic dispersion of international operations (PDIO).

In this study we follow a similar approach by measuring multinationality through three measures: (1) foreign sales/total sales (FSTS), (2) foreign profits/total profits (FPTP), and (3) foreign assets/total assets (FATA). A factor analysis of all observations is used to isolate the factor common to the three measures. Exhibit 7.1 reports the results. One common factor appears in the intercorrelations among the three variables, as the first eigenvalue alone exceeds the sum of the commonalities. The common factor is positively correlated with the three measures. The factor scores are used to measure the degree of multinationality of firms in the sample.

Measuring Corporate Reputation

The *Fortune* survey covers every industry group comprising four or more companies. The industry groups are based on categories established by the U.S. Office of Management and Budget (OMB). The survey asked executives, directors, and analysts in particular to rate a company on the following eight key attributes of reputation:

1. Quality of management
2. Quality of products/service offered
3. Innovativeness
4. Value as long-term investment
5. Soundness of financial position
6. Ability to attract/develop/keep talented people
7. Responsibility to the community/environment
8. Wise use of corporate assets

Rating were on a scale of 0 (poor) to 10 (excellent). The score met the multiple-constituency ecological model view of organizational effectiveness. For purposes of this study, the 1987 to 1990 *Fortune* magazine surveys were used. To obtain a unique configuration, a factor analysis is used to isolate the factor common to the eight measures of reputation. All the observations were subjected to factor analysis and one common factor was found to explain the intercorrelations among the eight individual measures. Exhibit 7.2 reports the results of the common factor analysis. One common factor appears to explain the intercorrelations among the eight variables, as the first eigenvalue alone exceeds the

Exhibit 7.1

Selected Statistics Related to a Common Factor Analysis of Three Measures of Multinationality for *Forbes'* The Most International 100 U.S. Firms for the 1987-1990 Period

1. **Eigenvalues of the Correlation Matrix:**

Eigenvalues	1	2	3
	1.8963	0.9169	0.1868

2. **Factor Pattern**

   FACTOR1

FS/TS	0.93853
FP/TP	0.40913
FA/TA	0.92089

3. **Final Communality Estimates: Total = 1.389626**

FS/TS	FP/TP	FA/TA
0.8808	0.16738	0.84804

4. **Standardized Scoring Coefficients**

   FACTOR1

FS/TS	0.49494
FP/TP	0.21575
FA/TA	0.48563

5. **Descriptive Statistics of the Common Factor Extracted from the Three Measures of Multinationality**

Maximum	201.059
Third Quartile	52.231
Median	41.50
First Quartile	30.648
Minimum	5.198
Mean	43.062

Variable Definitions
FS/TS = Foreign sales/total sales
FP/TP = Foreign profits/total profits
FA/TA = Foreign assets/total assets

Exhibit 7.2
Selected Statistics Related to a Common Factor Analysis of Measures of Reputation

1. **Eigenvalues of the Correlation Matrix:**

   Eigenvalues

1	2	3	4	5	6	7	8
6.7776	0.4596	0.3841	0.1347	0.1120	0.0549	0.0482	0.0331

2. **Factor Pattern**

   FACTOR1

R_1	0.9530	R_4	0.9645	R_7	0.8072
R_2	0.9180	R_5	0.8982	R_8	0.9479
R_3	0.8789	R_6	0.9805		

3. **Final Communality Estimates:**   Total = 1.389626

R_1	R_2	R_3	R_4	R_5	R_6	R_7	R_8
0.9093	0.8438	0.7726	0.9304	0.8069	0.9614	0.6516	0.8986

4. **Standardized Scoring Coefficients**

   FACTOR1

R_1	0.1407	R_4	0.1424	R_7	0.1191
R_2	0.1355	R_5	0.1326	R_8	0.1399
R_3	0.1297	R_6	0.1447		

5. **Descriptive Statistics of the Common Factor Extracted from the Eight Measures of Reputation**

Third Quartile	7.288
Median	6.618
First Quartile	6.105
Minimum	3.235
Mean	6.622

Variable Definitions
R_1 = Quality of management
R_2 = Quality of products/services
R_3 = Innovativeness
R_4 = Value as long-term investment
R_5 = Soundness of financial position
R_6 = Ability to attract, develop, and keep talented people
R_7 = Responsibility to the community and environment
R_8 = Wise use of corporate assets

sum of the commonalities. The common factor is significantly and positively correlated with the eight measures. The factor scores are used to measure the corporate reputation of firms.

Measuring Systematic Risk

The capital asset pricing model asserts that in equilibrium, and under certain conditions, the risk premium for an individual security, $E(\tilde{R}_i)$ − $E(\tilde{R}_F)$, is related to the risk premium of the market, $E(\tilde{R}_m)$ − $E(\tilde{R}_F)$, by the expression:

$$E(\tilde{R}_i) - E(\tilde{R}_F) = [E(\tilde{R}_m) - E(\tilde{R}_F)]\beta i$$

where:

$E(\tilde{R}_F)$ = risk-free rate

$E(\tilde{R}_m)$ = expected return on a market factor

$\beta i = \text{cov } (\tilde{R}_i, \tilde{R}_m)/\text{var}(\tilde{R}_m)$

βi is a measure of the systematic or nondiversifiable risk. Its estimation is operationally possible using the one-factor market model, which asserts a linear relationship between the rate of return on security i, R_{it}, and the market rate of return, R_{mt}, for a period t. It is expressed in this study as follows:

$$r_{it} = \alpha_i + \beta r_{mt} + e_{it}$$
$$E\{e_{it}\} = O$$
$$E\{e_{it}^2\} = N^o$$
$$E\{e_{it} \cdot e_{ik}\} = O, \forall k \neq t$$
$$E\{e_{st} \cdot e_{it}\} = O, \forall s \neq i$$
$$E\{In\{r_m^2\} \cdot e_{it}\} = O$$

where:

r_{it} = continuously compounded rate of return of security i at period t

$= \log_e(l + R_{it})$

$= \log_e[(P_t + D_t)/P_{t-1}]$

R_{it} = noncompounded single period return of security i in period t

r_m = market factor in period t log e

e_{it} = logarithm of the residual term

D_{it} = cash dividend per share

$\propto_i, \beta_i$ = parameters of the least-squares regression

r_{it} is used instead of R_{it} because it is admitted that, first, r_{it} has fewer outliers in its relative frequency distribution and therefore will yield more efficient risk statistics than R_{it}, and second, r_{it} is distributed more symmetrically than the positively skewed R_{it} variable. Besides, the results of the model are not changed by restating them in terms of r_{it} instead of R_{it}.

Measuring the Investment Opportunity Set

Because the investment opportunity set is not observable there has not been a consensus on an appropriate proxy variable. Similar to Smith and Watts[28] and Gaver and Gaver,[29] we use an ensemble of variables to measure the investment opportunity set. The three measures of the investment opportunity set used are: market-to-book assets (MASS), market to book equity (MQV), and the earnings/price ratio (EP). These variables are defined as follows:

MASS = [Assets−Total Common Equity+Shares Outstanding*Share Closing Price]/Assets

MV = [Shares Outstanding*Share Closing Price/Total Common Equity

EP = [Primary EPS before Extraordinary Items]/Share Closing Price

The results of a factor analysis of the three measures of the investment opportunity set are shown in Exhibit 7.3. One common factor appears to explain the intercorrelations among the three individual measures. Based on these factor scores, high-growth firms are chosen from the top 25 percent of the distribution scores while low-growth firms are chosen from the bottom 25 percent of the distribution factor scores. The two groups are used for testing the second hypothesis.

Exhibit 7.3

Selected Statistics Related to a Common Factor Analysis of Three Measures of the Investment Opportunity Set for *Forbes'* The Most International 100 U.S. Firms

1. **Eigenvalues of the Correlation Matrix: Total = 3   Avenue = 1**

Eigenvalue	1	2	3
	1.0540	0.9868	0.9592

2. **Factor Pattern**

FACTOR1

MASS	0.62821
MQV	0.66411
EP	0.46722

3. **Final Communality Estimates: Total = 1.053994**

MASS	MQV	EP
0.394651	0.441045	0.218299

4. **Standardized Scoring Coefficients**

FACTOR1

MASS	0.59603
MQV	0.63009
EP	0.44329

5. **Descriptive Statistics of the Common Factor Extracted from the Three Measures of the Investment Opportunity**

Maximum	9.3595
Third Quartile	3.2200
Median	2.0450
First Quartile	1.5085
Minimum	2.5209
Mean	1.9812

Exhibit 7.4
Summary Statistics for Empirical Variables

Panel A: Distributional Characteristics

Variables	Mean	Median	Range
BETA	1.009	1.004	0.106
MULTY	54.32	51.27	319.2
LEV	0.354	0.374	1.704
SIZE	16438	6175	136404
VROA	1.116	0.120	8.13
REP	6.622	6.614	5.78

Panel B: Pearson Correlation Among Regression Variables

	BETA	**MULTY**	**LEV**	**SIZE**	**VROA**	**REP**
BETA	1.000					
MULTY	0.123	1.000				
LEV	0.492[a]	0.089[b]	1.000			
SIZE	-0.158	-0.084[b]	-0.447[a]	1.000		
VROA	0.279[a]	0.026	0.268[a]	-0.201[a]	1.000	
REP	0.650[a]	-0.050	0.305[a]	-0.078	0.0564	1.000

[a]Significant at the 0.01 level.
[b]Significant at the 0.05 level.
Variable Definitions
BETA   = Systematic risk
MULTY = Index of multinationality
LEV   = Leverage ratio
VROA = Variance of return in assets
SIZE   = Size
REP   = Index of reputation

RESULTS

The Association of Multinationality with Systematic Risk

Exhibit 7.4 contains the descriptive statistics for the total sample for all the variables as well as the Pearson correlation coefficients among the regression variables. Exhibit 7.5 presents the estimated coefficients and t-statistics from the estimation of equation (1). As shown in Exhibit 7.4, the null hypothesis is rejected for α_1. Consistent with expectation, the multinationality score is significant and positive. All the control variables (REP, VROA, LEV, and SIZE) are significant and positive. The estimate of α_1 indicates that an increase of, say, 10 percent in the multinationality score is associated with a 0.00001 increase in BETA. The results show that the systematic risk of U.S. multinational firms is positively related to the level of multinationality after controlling for corporate reputation and other factors known to be associated with systematic risk.

Growth Opportunities Effect

Previous research has shown multinationality to be instead negatively related to systematic risk.[30] The difference in the results is attributed to a failure in considering the difference in the growth opportunities of firms in the sample, as measured by the investment opportunity set. Exhibit 7.5 shows the estimated coefficients and t-statistics from the estimation of equation (1) for both a high-investment opportunity set subsample and a low-investment opportunity set subsample.

As shown in Exhibit 7.6, the coefficient in the multinationality score is significant and negative for the high-investment opportunity set subsample and significant and positive for the low-investment subsample. All the control variables are, as expected, significant and positive for both groups of firms. The results indicate that increases in multinationality are associated with an increase in systematic risk for low-investment opportunity set firms and a decrease in systematic risk for high-investment opportunities set. It is the presence of strong growth opportunities that leads to a negative association between systematic risk and multinationality.

CONCLUSIONS AND IMPLICATIONS

The study examines the association between the level of multinationality of U.S. multinational firms and systematic risk as measured by the market model beta. Unlike previous studies, the results of this study show that systematic risk is positively related to the level of multinationality. However, a consideration of the growth opportunities of firms, as measured by the investment opportunity set, shows that the relation

Exhibit 7.5

Results of Pooled Time-Series Cross-Sectional Association Regression of Systematic Risk and Multinationality and Selected Variables

	Coefficients
INTERCEPT	-0.1182[2]
	(-18.477)[a]
MULTY[1]	0.0001
	(6.769)[a]
REP	0.003
	(5.189)[a]
VROA	0.0008
	(5.305)[a]
LEV	0.0275
	(7.265)[a]
SIZE	0.009
	(16.422)[a]
ADJUSTED R²	57.07%
n =	322

[1]*Variable Definitions*
MULTY = Index of multinationality
REP   = Index of reputation
VROA = Variance of return in assets
LEV   = Leverage ratio
SIZE = Firm size computed as log of total assets
[2]The regression is OLS. *t*-statistics are shown in parentheses based upon the White[31] corrected standard errors.
[a]Significant at the 1 percent level for the one-tailed test.

Exhibit 7.6

Relation between Systematic Risk and Multinationality and Selected Variables for High- and Low-Investment Opportunity Set

	High Investment Opportunity Set	**Low Investment Opportunity Set**
INTERCEPT	-0.058	-0.082
	(-5.183)[a]	(-12.549)[a]
MULTY	-0.000017	0.0001
	(-5.380)[a]	(4.744)[a]
REP	0.0046	0.001
	(3.424)[a]	(4.540)[a]
VROA	0.0003	0.0003
	(8.650)[a]	(3.070)[a]
LEV	0.022	0.013[a]
	(3.482)[a]	(3.552)[a]
SIZE	0.003	0.007
	(2.730)[a]	(13.895)[a]
ADJUSTED R²	49.29%	72.74%
n =	89	89

[a]Significant at the 0.01 level.

is negative for high-investment opportunity set firms and positive for low-investment opportunity set firms. The increase in systematic risk, following an increase in multinationality, is the result of lack of growth opportunities. It is when multinationality is associated with high-growth opportunities that systematic risk is negatively related to international diversification.

NOTES

1. S. R. Goldberg and F. L. Heflin, "The Association between the Level of International Diversification and Risk," *Journal of International Financial Management and Accounting* 6 (1995): 1–25.

2. J. S. Hughes, D. E. Logue, and R. J. Sweeney, "Corporate International Diversification and Market Assigned Measures of Risk and Diversification," *Journal of Financial and Quantitative Analysis* 10 (November 1975): 627–637.

3. T. Agmon and D. R. Lessard, "Investor Recognition of Corporate International Diversification," *Journal of Finance* 32 (September): 1049–1055.

4. J. Madura and L. C. Rose, "Impact of International Sales Degree and Diversity on Corporate Risk," *International Trade Journal* (Spring 1989): 261–276.

5. A. R. Rugman, "Foreign Operations and the Stability of U.S. Corporate Earnings: Risk Reduction by International Diversification," *Journal of Finance* (March 1977), pp. 233–234.

6. Goldberg and Heflin, "The Association between the Level of International Diversification and Risk," 1–25.

7. A. Belkaoui, "Accounting Determinants of Systematic Risk in Canadian Common Stocks: A Multivariate Approach," *Accounting and Business Research* 33 (Winter 1978): 3–10.

8. R. G. Bowman, "The Theoretical Relationship between Systematic Risk and Financial (Accounting) Variables," *Journal of Finance* 34 (June 1979): 617–630.

9. N. C. Hill and B. K. Stone, "Accounting Betas, Systematic Operating Risk, and Financial Leverage: A Risk-Composition Approach to the Determinants of Systematic Risk," *Journal of Financial and Quantitative Analysis* 15 (September 1980): 595–637.

10. W. Beaver, P. Kettler, and M. Scholes, "The Association between Market Determined and According Determined Risk Measures," *The Accounting Review* 45 (October 1970): 654–682.

11. John H. Dunning, *Explaining International Production* (London: Unwin Hyman, 1988).

12. John H. Dunning, "The Eclectic Paradigm of International Production: A Restatement and Some Possible Extensions," *Journal of International Business Studies* 19, no. 1 (1988): 1–32.

13. S. Myers, "Determinants of Corporate Borrowing," *Journal of Financial Economics* 5 (1977), 147–175.

14. W. C. Kester, "Today's Options for Tomorrow's Growth," *Harvard Business Review* (March-April 1984): 153–160.

15. Belkaoui, "Accounting Determinants of Systematic Risk in Canadian Common Stocks: A Multivariate Approach," 3–10.

16. Bowman, "The Theoretical Relationship between Systematic Risk and Financial (Accounting) Variables," 617–630.

17. Hill and Stone, "Accounting Betas, Systematic Operating Risk, and Financial Leverage: A Risk-Composition Approach to the Determinants of Systematic Risk," 595–637.

18. Beaver, Kettler, and Scholes, "The Association between Market Determined and Accounting Determined Risk Measures," 654–682.

19. Goldberg and Heflin, "The Association between the Level of International Diversification and Risk," 1–25.

20. A. M. Spence, *Market Signaling: Information Transfer in Hiring and Related Screening Process* (Cambridge, MA: Harvard University Press, 1974).

21. C. Forbrum and M. Shanley, "What's in a Name? Reputational Building and Corporate Strategy," *Academy of Management Journal* 33 (1990): 233–258.

22. Ahmed Belkaoui, "Organizational Effectiveness, Social Performance and Economic Performance," *Research in Corporate Social Performance and Policy* 12 (1992): 143–155.

23. Ahmed Riahi-Belkaoui and E. Pavlik, "Asset Management Performance and Reputation Building for Large U.S. Firms," *British Journal of Management* 2 (1991): 231–238.

24. John H. Dunning, "Reappraising the Eclectic Paradigm in an Age of Alliance Capitalism," *Journal of International Business Studies* 26 (1995): 461–492.

25. John M. Stopford and Louis T. Wells, *Managing the Multinational Enterprise* (New York: Basic Books, 1972).

26. Howard V. Perlmutter, "The Tortuous Evaluation of the Multinational Corporation," *Columbia Journal of World Business* 4 (January-February 1969): 9–18.

27. D. Sullivan, "Measuring the Degree of Internationalization of a Firm," *Journal of International Business Studies* 25 (1994): 325–342.

28. C. W. Smith and R. L. Watts, "The Investment Opportunity Set and Corporate Financing, Dividend and Compensation Policies," *Journal of Financial Economics* 32 (1992): 263–292.

29. J. J. Gaver and K. M. Gaver, "Additional Evidence on the Association between the Investment Opportunity Set and Corporate Financing, Dividend, and Compensation Policies," *Journal of Accounting and Economics* 16 (1993): 125–160.

30. Goldberg and Heflin, "The Association between the Level of International Diversification and Risk," 1–25.

31. H. A. White, "Heteroskedasticity-Consistent Covariance Matrix Estimator and a Direct Test for Heteroskedasticity," *Econometrika* 10 (1980): 817–838.

SELECTED READINGS

Agmon, T., and D. R. Lessard. "Investor Recognition of Corporate International Diversification." *Journal of Finance* 32 (September 1977): 1049–1055.

Beatty, R. P., and J. R. Ritter. "Investment Banking, Reputation, and Underpricing of Initial Public Offerings." *Journal of Financial Economics* 15 (1986): 213–232.

Beaver, W., P. Kettler, and M. Scholes. "The Association between Market Determined and Accounting Determined Risk Measures." *Accounting Review* 45 (October 1970): 654–682.

Belkaoui, A. "Accounting Determinants of Systematic Risk in Canadian Common Stocks: A Multivariate Approach." *Accounting and Business Research* 33 (Winter 1978): 3–10.

Belkaoui, Ahmed. "Organizational Effectiveness, Social Performance and Economic Performance." *Research in Corporate Social Performance and Policy* 12 (1992): 143–155.

Belsley, D., E. Kuh, and R. Welsch. *Regression Diagnostics: Identifying Influential Data and Sources of Collinearity.* New York: Wiley, 1980.

Bernard, V. "Cross-Sectional Dependence and Problems in Inference in Market-Based Accounting Research." *Journal of Accounting Research* (Spring 1987): 1–48.

Bowman, R. G. "The Theoretical Relationship between Systematic Risk and Financial (Accounting) Variables." *Journal of Finance* 34 (June 1979): 617–630.

Dunning, John H. *Explaining International Production.* London: Unwin Hyman, 1988.

———. "The Eclectic Paradigm of International Production: A Restatement and Some Possible Extensions." *Journal of International Business Studies* 19, no. 1: (1988): 1–32.

———. "Reappraising the Eclectic Paradigm in an Age of Alliance Capitalism." *Journal of International Business Studies* 26 (1995): 461–492.

Eiteman, D., and A. Stonehill. *Multinational Business Finance.* Boston: Addison, 1986.

Forbrum, C., and M. Shanley. "What's in a Name? Reputational Building and Corporate Strategy." *Academy of Management Journal* 33 (1990): 233–258.

Gaver, J. J., and K. M. Gaver. "Additional Evidence on the Association between the Investment Opportunity Set and Corporate Financing, Dividend, and Compensation Policies." *Journal of Accounting and Economics* 16 (1993): 125–160.

Goldberg, S. R., and F. L. Heflin. "The Association between the Level of International Diversification and Risk." *Journal of International Financial Management and Accounting* 6 (1995): 1–25.

Hill, N. C., and B. K. Stone. "Accounting Betas, Systematic Operating Risk, and Financial Leverage: A Risk-Composition Approach to the Determinants of Systematic Risk." *Journal of Financial and Quantitative Analysis* 15 (September 1980): 595–637.

Hughes, J. S., D. E. Logue, and R. J. Sweeney. "Corporate International Diversification and Market Assigned Measures of Risk and Diversification." *Journal of Financial and Quantitative Analysis* 10 (November 1975): 627–637.

Kester, W. C. "Today's Options for Tomorrow's Growth." *Harvard Business Review* (March-April 1984): 153–160.

Kogut, Bruce. "Foreign Direct Investment as a Sequential Process." In C. P. Kindelberger and D. B. Audretsch, eds. *The Multinational Corporation in the 1980s*. Cambridge, MA: MIT Press, 1983: 38–56.

Madura, J., and L. C. Rose. "Impact of International Sales Degree and Diversity on Corporate Risk." *International Trade Journal* (Spring 1989): 261–276.

Myers, S. "Determinants of Corporate Borrowing." *Journal of Financial Economics* 5 (1977): 147–175.

Perlmutter, Howard V. "The Tortuous Evaluation of the Multinational Corporation." *Columbia Journal of World Business* 4 (January-February 1969): 9–18.

Riahi-Belkaoui, Ahmed, and E. Pavlik. "Asset Management Performance and Reputation Building for Large U.S. Firms." *British Journal of Management* 2 (1991): 231–238.

Rugman, A. R. "Foreign Operations and the Stability of U.S. Corporate Earnings: Risk Reduction by International Diversification." *Journal of Finance* (March 1977): 233–234.

Smith, C. W., and R. L. Watts. "The Investment Opportunity Set and Corporate Financing, Dividend and Compensation Policies." *Journal of Financial Economics* 32 (1992): 263–292.

Spence, A. M. *Market Signaling: Information Transfer in Hiring and Related Screening Process*. Cambridge, MA: Harvard University Press, 1974.

Stopford, John M., and Louis T. Wells. *Managing the Multinational Enterprise*. New York: Basic Books, 1972.

Sullivan, D. "Measuring the Degree of Internationalization of a Firm." *Journal of International Business Studies* 25 (1994): 325–342.

White, H. A. "Heteroskedasticity-Consistent Covariance Matrix Estimator and a Direct Test for Heteroskedasticity." *Econometrika* 10 (1980): 817–838.

8

Profitability, Multinationality, and Investment Opportunity Set

INTRODUCTION

The firm may be viewed as a combination of assets-in-place and future investment options. The lower the proportion of firm value represented by assets-in-place, the higher the growth opportunities. Myers[1] describes these potential investment opportunities as call options whose values depend on the likelihood that management will exercise them. Like call options, the growth options represent real value to the firm.[2] These growth options are intangible assets that represent the investment opportunity set of a firm. Given that the market value of a firm is comprised of the value of assets-in-place and the present value of these growth opportunities, the difference in market values of firms implies a difference in the investment opportunity set. Firm-specific and economic-based variables are potential determinants of the cross-sectional differences in the investment opportunity set. This study considers the two firm variables of multinationality and profitability as determinants of the investment opportunity set. Accordingly, it examines the impact of multinationality and profitability on the investment opportunity set, conditioned by size and macroeconomic variables. The results, based on a sample of 600 firm-year observations from *Forbes'* Most International

100 American manufacturing and service firms from the 1987 to the 1992 period, indicate a significant positive relation with multinationality and profitability, inflation and GNP growth rate, and a negative relation with size and the index of business formation.

BACKGROUND AND HYPOTHESES

Profitability and the Investment Opportunity Set

Cross-sectional differences in the investment opportunity set lead to differences in the optimality of alternative financing, dividend, and compensation policies.[3,4] This is a verification of Myers'[5] prediction that the larger the proportion of firm value represented by growth options (i.e., the lower the assets-in-place), the lower the firm's leverage, and the higher its equity-to-value ratio. Like call options on securities, the investment opportunity set (or growth options) represents real value and profit potential to the firms that possess it.[6] Its value, estimated by a comparison of the capitalized value of the firm's current earnings stream and the market value of the firm's equity, is half or more of the market value of equity of many firms, and about 70 to 80 percent in industries with high demand volatility.[7] More recently, Pindyck[8] showed that the fraction of market value attributable to the value of capital in place should be only one-half or less for firms with reasonable demand volatility. He specifically argued that if the demand volatility is 0.2 or more, more than half of the firm's value is accounted for by its growth opportunities. Similarly, Miles[9] found that the beta of these growth options depends on the profitability of future investment, the quantity of future investments, and the firm's own instantaneous return variance. In addition, two seminal papers from financial economics combine to provide a theoretical framework for describing the investment opportunity set. Myers[10] depicts firm value as a combination of income-generating assets-in-place (Va) and growth opportunities (Vg).

$$V = Va + Vg$$

Firms with more assets-in-place have less of their value determined by growth opportunities and vice versa.

Myers' concept of firm value is consistent with that of Miller and Modigliani[11] (MM), who modeled the value of firm based upon (1) the market rate of return, (2) the earning power of assets-in-place, and (3) the opportunities for making additional investments in real assets that will yield more than the normal rate of return (i.e., growth opportunities). MM's equation (12) (using their notation) shows the value of the firm (*V*) at time 0:

$$V(0) = \frac{X(0)}{\rho} + \sum_{t=0}^{\infty} I(t) \times \frac{\rho^*(t) - \rho}{\rho} (1 + \rho)^{-(t+1)}$$

where $X(0)$ are earnings from assets-in-place, ρ is the cost of capital, ρ^* is some internal rate of return that exceeds ρ, and I is investment made at time t. The second right-hand-section term encompasses Myers' growth term (Vg) and is what is commonly called the investment opportunity set (IOS). Holding firm value constant, the two right-hand-section terms are inversely related. This is the "normal" view of growth firms, forgoing earnings from assets-in-place [$X(0)$] in the first term, by plowing them back into investment (I) in the second term. A recent example is the wireless communications industry during the 1980s, showing consistently depressed earnings (and losses) due to significant investments, which combined to result in rapidly increasing firm value. Since both the first and second right-hand-section terms should be correlated with firm value, they are correlated with each other. Accordingly:

H1: There is a positive relationship between the investment opportunity set and profitability.

Multinationality and the Investment Opportunity Set

The multinational firm is a collection of valuable options and generates profits that enhance its value.[12] The arbitrage benefits result from (a) the exploitation of various institutional imperfections; (b) timing options; (c) technology options; and (d) staging options.[13,14] Better financing bargains[15] as well as capital availability[16] are also possible through internationalization. In addition, multinational firms can achieve arbitrage benefits in financing cash flows by (a) exploiting financial bargains; (b) reducing taxes on financial flows; and (c) mitigating risks or shifting them to agents with a comparative advantage in bearing them.[17] This definition of multinationality as a collection of options and arbitrage benefits suggests a positive relation with growth options as defined by the investment opportunity set. More growth options are more likely to result from increased internationalization. Accordingly:

H2: There is a positive relation between the investment opportunity set and multinationality.

METHODS

Data Analysis and Sample

A multiple regression was used to test the relationship between the investment opportunity set on one hand, and profitability and multinationality on the other hand. The model's control variables are size, annual percentage changes in gross national product (GNP), annual inflation rate, and the index of business formation.

The sample consisted of all the firms included in *Forbes'* Most International 100 American manufacturing and service firms for the 1987 to 1992 period.

Measuring Multinationality

Previous research has attempted to measure three attributes of the degree of multinationality:

1. *Performance*—in terms of what goes on overseas[18]
2. *Structure*—in terms of how resources are used overseas[19]
3. *Attitude or conduct*—in terms of what is top management orientation[20]

Nine measures were identified to include: (1) foreign sales as a percentage of total sales (FSTS), (2) research and development intensity (RDI), (3) advertising intensity (AI), (4) export sales as a percentage of total sales (ESTS), (5) foreign profits as a percentage of total profits (FPTP), (6) foreign assets over total assets (FATA), (7) overseas subsidiaries as a percentage of total subsidiaries (OSTS), (8) top management's international experience (TMIE), and (9) psychic dispersion of international operations (PDIO).[21] Of these nine measures, an item-total analysis showed the five variables of FSTS, FATA, OSTS, PDIO, and TMIE to have a high reliability in the construction of a homogeneous measure of multinationality.

We follow a similar approach in this study, using an ensemble of variables to measure multinationality. Three measures of multinationality generally available are used in this study: foreign sales/total sales

Exhibit 8.1
Descriptive Statistics and Correlations of Three Measures of Multinationality for *Forbes'* The Most International 100 U.S. Firms for the 1987-1992 Period

Panel A: Descriptive Statistics

	FP/TP[a]	FS/TS[b]	FA/TA[c]
Maximum	914.3	93	91
Third Quartile	61.9	47.4	41.4
Median	41.3	36.7	30.5
First Quartile	25	25.7	22.6
Minimum	0.2	6.6	2.7
Mean	52.81	37.45	39.92

Panel B: Correlations

	FP/TP	FS/TS	FA/TA
FP/TP	1.000		
FS/TS	0.280	1.000	
FA/TA	0.034	0.193*	1.000

*Denotes *p*-value < 0.05.
Variable Definitions
FP/TP = Foreign profits/total profits
FS/TS = Foreign sales/total sales
FA/TA = Foreign assets/total assets

(FSTS), foreign profits/total profits (FPTP), and foreign assets/total assets (FATA). Descriptive statistics and correlations among the three measures of multinationality are shown in Exhibit 8.1. Correlations among the variables are positive, and with one exception, all significant. The non-significant correlation is between FPTP and FATA. The low correlations between FPTP, FSTS, and FATA indicate that each variable can make a unique contribution as a measure of multinationality. To obtain a unique contribution, a factor analysis is used to isolate the factor common to the three measures of multinationality. All the observations were subjected to factor analysis and one common factor was found to explain the intercorrelations among the three individual measures.[22] Exhibit 8.2 reports the results of the common factor analysis. One common factor appears to explain the intercorrelations among the three variables, as the first eigenvalue alone exceeds the sum of the commonalities. The com-

Exhibit 8.2

Selected Statistics Related to a Common Factor Analysis of Three Measures of Multinationality for *Forbes'* The Most International 100 U.S. Firms for the 1987-1992 Period

1. Eigenvalues of the Correlation Matrix:

Eigenvalues	1	2	3
	1.3615	0.9680	0.6705

2. Factor Pattern

    FACTOR1

FS/TS	0.80529
FP/TP	0.50172
FA/TA	0.67918

3. Final Communality Estimates: Total = 1.361489

FS/TS	FP/TP	FA/TA
0.648491	0.251718	0.461280

4. Standardized Scoring Coefficients

    FACTOR1

FS/TS	0.59148
FP/TP	0.36850
FA/TA	0.49885

5. Descriptive Statistics of the Common Factor Extracted from the Three Measures of Multinationality

Maximum	2039.24
Third Quartile	74.70
Median	57.03
First Quartile	4 0.76
Minimum	5.17
Mean	64.35

mon factor is significantly and positively correlated with the three measures. As pointed out earlier, based on these factor scores, high-multinationality firms were chosen from the top 25 percent of the distribution factor scores while low-multinationality firms were chosen from the bottom 25 percent of the distribution factor scores.

Measuring the Investment Opportunity Set

Because the investment opportunity set is not observable there has not been a consensus on an appropriate proxy variable. Similar to Smith and Watts[23] and Gaver and Gaver,[24] we use an ensemble of variables to measure the investment opportunity set. The three measures of the investment opportunity set used are: market-to-book assets (MASS), market-to-book equity (MQV), and the earnings/price ratio (EP). These variables are defined as follows:

$MASS$ = [Assets − Total Common Equity + Shares Outstanding*Share Closing Price]/Assets

MQV = [Shares Outstanding*Share Closing Price]/Total Common Equity

EP = [Primary EPS before Extraordinary Items]/Share Closing Price

Descriptive statistics and correlations among the three measures of the investment opportunity set are shown in Exhibit 8.3. Correlations among the three variables are significant. The low correlations indicate that each variable makes a unique contribution as a measure of the investment opportunity set. The results of the factor analysis are shown in Exhibit 8.4. One common factor appears to explain the intercorrelations among the three individual measures. As pointed out earlier, based on these factor scores, high-growth firms were chosen from the top 25 percent of the distribution scores while low-growth firms were chosen from the bottom 25 percent of the distribution factor scores.

Profitability

The central profitability measure used in this study is a time series of the rate of return on assets over the 1987–1992 period. It is computed as follows:

Exhibit 8.3
Descriptive Statistics and Correlation of Three Measures of the
Investment Opportunity Set for *Forbes'* **The Most International 100 U.S.**
Firms for the 1987-1992 Period

Panel A: Descriptive Statistics

	MASS	MQV	EP
Maximum	6.4943	60	0.5175
Third Quartile	1.8556	3.1851	0.1081
Median	1.2905	1.9090	0.0713
First Quartile	1.0618	1.2666	0.0482
Minimum	0.8745	4.3333	2.1536
Mean	0.3081	2.7020	0.0638

Panel B: Correlation

	MASS	MQV	EP
MASS	1.000		
MQV	0.0399*	1.000	
EP	0.0158*	0.0230*	1.000

*Denotes p-value < 0.05.
Variable Definitions
MASS = Market-to-book assets
MQV = Market-to-book equity
EP   = Earnings/price ratio

Rate of Return on Assets (ROA) = Net Profit/Total Assets

Conditioning Firm and Economy Variables

The logarithm of total assets, annual percentage change in gross national product and inflation rate, and an index of net business formation were used as conditioning variables. The logarithm of total assets was used to control for size. The annual percentage change in gross national product and in inflation rate as well as the index of business formation controlled for changes in growth opportunities related to major external

Exhibit 8.4

Selected Statistics Related to a Common Factor Analysis of Three Measures of the Investment Opportunity Set for *Forbes'* The Most International 100 U.S. Firms for the 1987-1992 Period

1. Eigenvalues of the Correlation Matrix: Total = 3 Average = 1

Eigenvalues	1	2	3
	1.0540	0.9868	0.9592

2. Factor Pattern

    FACTOR1

MASS	0.62821
MQV	0.66411
EP	0.46722

3. Final Communality Estimates: Total = 1.053994

MASS	MQV	EP
0.394651	0.441045	0.218299

4. Standardized Scoring Coefficients

    FACTOR1

MASS	0.59603
MQV	0.63009
EP	0.44329

5. Descriptive Statistics of the Common Factor Extracted from the Three Measures of the Investment Opportunity

Maximum	9.3595
Third Quartile	3.2200
Median	2.0450
First Quartile	1.5085
Minimum	2.5209
Mean	1.9812

Exhibit 8.5
Regression Results for Rate of Return on Assets

Sources	Coefficient	P
Intercept	74.458	2.780*
Index of Multinationality	0.8942	2.358*
Rate of Return on Assets	19.273	5.085*
Conditioning Variables		
Size (Log of Assets)	-0.421	-2.462*
Annual Percentage Changes in GNP	1.2052	2.133**
Annual Percentage Changes in Inflation	3.1233	2.589*
Index of Business Formation	-0.6917	-2.576*
F	13.607*	
R2	0.2418	

*Significant at the 0.01 level.
**Denotes p-value < 0.05.

shifts in aggregate demand and provided an analysis conditioned by macroeconomic variables. The macroeconomic variables were obtained from the *Economic Report of the President*.[25]

RESULTS AND DISCUSSION

Exhibit 8.5 presents the results of the regression between the investment opportunity set index on one hand and the index of multinationality and rate of return on assets on the other hand. Size, annual percentage changes in GNP and inflation, and the index of business formation are used as conditioning variables. The overall model is significant ($F = 13.607$, $p = 0.001$) and explains 24.18 percent of the variations in the investment opportunity set index. As hypothesized, both the index of multinationality and the rate of return on assets are significantly and positively related to the index representing the investment opportunity set. In addition, all the conditioning variables are significantly related to the investment opportunity set.[26]

The results point to the salient role of multinationality and profitability in creating growth opportunities to the firm. Basically, the higher the multinationality and the profitability, the higher the growth opportunities to the firm as defined by the investment opportunity set. Multinationality presents the ideal context for the creation of valuable options and benefits that define the growth opportunities of the investment opportunity set. Similarly, profitability defines the quality and quantity of future investments that also define the growth opportunities of the investment opportunity set.

Future research needs to correct for some of the limitations of this study. First, the sample may not be limited to the *Forbes'* Most International firms. Second, other proxy variables for multinationality and the investment opportunity set may be used. Finally, other explanatory variables besides multinationality and profitability should be included as potential determinants of the investment opportunity set.

NOTES

1. S. Myers, "Determinants of Corporate Borrowing," *Journal of Financial Economics* 5 (1977): 147–175.

2. W. C. Kester, "Today's Options for Tomorrow's Growth," *Harvard Business Review* (March-April 1984): 153–160.

3. J. J. Gaver and K. M. Gaver, "Additional Evidence on the Association between the Investment Opportunity Set and Corporate Financing, Dividend, and Compensation Policies," *Journal of Accounting and Economics* (1993): 125–160.

4. C. W. Smith and R. L. Watts, "The Investment Opportunity Set and Corporate Financing, Dividend and Compensation Policies," *Journal of Financial Economics* 32 (1992): 263–292.

5. Myers, "Determinants of Corporate Borrowing," 147–175.

6. Kester, "Today's Options for Tomorrow's Growth," 153–160.

7. W. C. Kester, "An Options Approach to Corporate Finance." In E. Altman, ed., *Handbook of Corporate Finance*, 2d ed. (New York: Wiley, 1986).

8. R. Pindyck, "Irreversible Investment, Capacity Choice, and the Value of the Firm," *American Economic Review* (1988): 969–985.

9. J. A. Miles, "Growth Options and the Real Determinants of Systematic Risk," *Journal of Business Finance and Accounting* 13 (1986): 95–106.

10. Myers, "Determinants of Corporate Borrowing," 147–175.

11. Merton H. Miller and Franco Modigliani, "Dividend Policy, Growth, and the Valuation of Shares," *Journal of Business* (1961): 441–433.

12. George P. Tsetsekos, "Multinationality and Common Stock Offering," *Journal of International Financial Management and Accounting* 3 (1991): 1–16.

13. John H. Dunning, "Reappraising the Eclectic Paradigm in an Age of Alliance Capitalism," *Journal of International Business Studies* 26 (1995): 461–492.

14. Bruce Kogut, "Foreign Direct Investment as a Sequential Process." In C. P. Kindelberger and D. B. Audretsch, eds., *The Multinational Corporation in the 1980s* (Cambridge, MA: MIT Press, 1983): 38–56.

15. F. Giavazzi and A. Giovannini, *Limiting Exchange Rate Flexibility: The European Monetary System* (Cambridge, MA: MIT Press, 1989).

16. D. Eiteman and A. Stonehill, *Multinational Business Finance* (Boston: Addison-Wesley, 1986).

17. Tsetsekos, "Multinationality and Common Stock Offering," 1–16.

18. Dunning, "Reappraising the Eclectic Paradigm in an Age of Alliance Capitalism," 461–492.

19. John M. Stopford and Louis T. Wells, *Managing the Multinational Enterprise* (New York: Basic Books, 1972).

20. H. V. Perlmutter, "The Tortuous Evaluation of the Multinational Corporation," *Columbia Journal of World Business* 4 (1969): 9–18.

21. Daniel Sullivan, "Measuring the Degree of Internationalization of a Firm," *Journal of International Business Studies* 25 (1994): 325–342.

22. H. H. Hartman, *Modern Factor Analysis*, 3rd ed. (Chicago: University of Chicago Press, 1976).

23. Smith and Watts, "The Investment Opportunity Set and Corporate Financing, Dividend and Compensation Policies," 263–292.

24. Gaver and Gaver, "Additional Evidence on the Association between the Investment Opportunity Set and Corporate Financing, Dividend, and Compensation Policies," 125–160.

25. *Economic Report of the President* (Washington, DC: U.S. Government Printing Office, 1995).

26. The exchange rate, added as a conditioning variable, was not significant.

SELECTED READINGS

Dunning, John H. "Reappraising the Eclectic Paradigm in an Age of Alliance Capitalism." *Journal of International Business Studies* 26 (1995): 461–492.

Economic Report of the President. Washington, DC: U.S. Government Printing Office, 1995.

Eiteman, D., and A. Stonehill. *Multinational Business Finance.* Boston: Addison-Wesley, 1986.

Gaver, J. J., and K. M. Gaver. "Additional Evidence on the Association between the Investment Opportunity Set and Corporate Financing, Dividend, and Compensation Policies." *Journal of Accounting and Economics* (1993): 125–160.

Giavazzi, E., and A. Giovannini. *Limiting Exchange Rate Flexibility: The European Monetary System.* Cambridge, MA: MIT Press, 1989.

Hartman, H. H. *Modern Factor Analysis*, 3rd ed. Chicago: University of Chicago Press, 1976.

Kester, W. C. "Today's Options for Tomorrow's Growth." *Harvard Business Review* (March-April 1984): 153–160.

———. "An Options Approach to Corporate Finance." In E. Altman, ed. *Handbook of Corporate Finance*, 2d ed. New York: Wiley, 1986.

Kogut, Bruce. "Foreign Direct Investment as a Sequential Process." In C. P. Kindelberger and D. B. Audretsch eds. *The Multinational Corporation in the 1980s.* Cambridge, MA: MIT Press, 1983: 38–56.

———. "Designing Global Strategies: Profiting from Operational Flexibility." *Sloan Management Review* (1985): 27–38.

Miles, J. A. "Growth Options and the Real Determinants of Systematic Risk." *Journal of Business Finance and Accounting* 13 (1986): 95–106.

Miller, Merton H., and Franco Modigliani. "Dividend Policy, Growth, and the Valuation of Shares." *Journal of Business* (1961): 441–433.

Myers, S. "Determinants of Corporate Borrowing." *Journal of Financial Economics* 5 (1977): 147–175.

Perlmutter, H. V. "The Tortuous Evaluation of the Multinational Corporation." *Columbia Journal of World Business* 4 (1969): 9–18.

Pindyck, R. "Uncertainty and Exhaustible Resource Market." *Journal of Political Economy* (1980): 1203–1225.

———. "Irreversible Investment, Capacity Choice, and the Value of the Firm." *American Economic Review* (1988): 969–985.

Smith, C. W., and R. L. Watts. "The Investment Opportunity Set and Corporate Financing, Dividend and Compensation Policies." *Journal of Financial Economics* 32 (1992): 263–292.

Stopford, John M., and Louis T. Wells, *Managing the Multinational Enterprise.* New York: Basic Books, 1972.

Sullivan, Daniel. "Measuring the Degree of Internationalization of a Firm." *Journal of International Business Studies* 25 (1994): 325–342.

Tsetsekos, George P. "Multinationality and Common Stock Offering." *Journal of International Financial Management and Accounting* 3 (1991): 1–16.

Investment Opportunity Set and Corporate Financing: The Contingency of Multinationality

INTRODUCTION

The study employs a contingency perspective to examine the association between the investment opportunity set and corporate financing given different levels of multinationality. Theories of corporate financing have often emphasized the various roles of debt, including the tax advantage of debt,[1] choice of debt level to signal firm quality,[2,3] use of debt as an antitakeover device,[4] agency costs of debt,[5,6] and usefulness of debt for restricting a managerial discretion.[7] There is, however, no consensus about which determinants have an impact on the capital structure decision, or how they affect performance.[8,9] We agree that Barton and Gordon's[10] suggestion to employ a managerial perspective will add to the understanding of the capital structure decision.[11]

Specifically, we test whether the investment opportunity set is associated with corporate financing, and whether such association varies over firms with different levels of multinationality. The analysis is conducted at the firm level to allow for more powerful tests than at the industry level. In addition, composite measures of multinationality and the investment opportunity set are used to reduce classification errors in both variables. Specifically, a common factor analysis is used to create an index of multinationality (IOM) and an index of investment opportunity set (IOS). A covariance analysis of the market debt/equity of our sample firms suggests that the investment opportunity set creates different corporate financing in firms that vary in terms of multinationality after controlling for size, changes in GNP, inflation rate, and the index of business formation. In general, the findings support a contingency view of the association between the investment opportunity set and corporate financing.

BACKGROUND AND HYPOTHESES

Corporate Financing and the Investment Opportunity Set

The firms may be viewed as a combination of assets-in-place and future investment options. The lower the proportion of firm value represented by assets-in-place, the higher the proportion of firm value represented by growth opportunities. Myers[12] argued that for firms with growth opportunities or investment opportunity sets, the existence of risky debt, maturing after the investment option, causes the firm to forgo profitable investment, resulting in an underinvestment scenario. Growth firms tend to issue less debt than firms without growth opportunities. As a result, prior empirical research in finance and accounting examining the cross-sectional differences in major corporate policy decisions relied on contracting cost explanations and presented empirical evidence regarding the relationship between the investment opportunity set and financing policies.[13,14] More evidence is provided in this chapter.

H1: Growth firms have lower debt/equity than nongrowth firms.

Corporate Financing and Multinationality

Firms make investment in physical and human capital internationally thus determining level of multinationality. Myers' theory can be expanded to explain how international conditions can lead a multinational corporation to either accelerate the shift from one financing method to the next or rearrange the pecking order.[15] A situation characterized by lower country risk, higher interest rates, expected strength of host country currency, blocked funds, and lower withholding and corporate taxes calls for a higher amount of external debt financing by the parent and a lower amount by the subsidiary, and vice versa. Where internal funding is not available to the parent, the same conditions that encourage use of debt financing by the subsidiary will result in a more debt-intensive capital structure for the multinational firm.[16] Another alternative explanation for the higher debt of multinational firms is that multinational firms, having diversified cash flows, may be able to support more debt. Accordingly:

> **H2**: High-multinationality firms have higher debt/equity ratios than low-multinationality firms.

METHODOLOGY

Data Analysis

Covariance analysis was used to test the overall relationship between: (1) corporate financing and the investment opportunity set, (2) corporate financing and multinationality, and (3) the interaction of corporate financing, multinationality, and the investment opportunity set. The control variables are size, annual percentage changes in gross national product (GNP) as well as inflation rate, and the index of business formation.

Selection of Firms

The population consists of firms included in *Forbes'* Most International 100 American manufacturing and service firms for the 1987 to 1992 period. The sample consists of firms that are either high on multinationality and investment opportunity set or low on both variables. Common factor analyses were used to create an *index of multinationality* (IOM) and an *index of investment opportunity set* (IOS). Firm-year observations in the top quartiles of both indices were partioned in a high-growth, high-multinationality subsample, and firm-year observations in the bottom quartile of both indices were classified in a low-growth, low-multinationality subsample. The first subsample of high-growth, high-multinationality included eighty firm-year observations while the second sample of low-growth, low-multinationality included 121 firm-year observations.

Measuring Multinationality

Previous research has attempted to measure the following attributes of multinationality:

1. *Performance*—in terms of what goes on overseas[17]
2. *Structure*—in terms of resources used overseas[18]
3. *Attitude or Conduct*—in terms of what is top management's orientation[19]

Sullivan[20] developed nine measures of which five were shown to have a high reliability in the construction of a homogeneous measure of nationality: (1) foreign sales as a percentage of total sales (FSTS), (2) foreign assets over total assets (FATA), (3) overseas subsidiaries as a percentage of total subsidiaries (OSTS), (4) top management's international experience (TMIE), and (5) psychic dispersion of international operations (PDIO).

In this study we follow a similar approach by measuring multinationality through three measures: (1) foreign sales/total sales (FSTS), (2) foreign profits/total profits (FPTP), and (3) foreign assets/total assets (FATA).

Descriptive statistics and correlations among the three multinationality measures are shown in Exhibit 9.1. Correlations among the variables are positive, and with one exception, all significant. The nonsignificant correlation is between FPTP and FATA. The low correlations between FPTP, FSTS, and FATA indicate that each variable can make a unique contribution as a multinationality measure. Thus, a factor analysis of all observations is used to isolate the factor common to the three measures. Exhibit 9.2 reports the results. One common factor appears in the intercorrelations among the three variables, as the first eigenvalue value alone exceeds the sum of the commonalities. The common factor is significantly positively correlated with the three measures. As pointed out earlier, based on these factor scores, high-multinationality firms were chosen from the top 25 percent of the distribution factor scores while low-multinationality firms were chosen from the bottom 25 percent of the distribution factor scores.

Measuring the Investment Opportunity Set

Because the investment opportunity set is not observable there has not been a consensus in an appropriate proxy variable. Similar to Smith and Watts[21] and Gaver and Gaver,[22] we use a set of three variables to measure the investment opportunity set: market-to-book assets (MASS), market-

Exhibit 9.1
Descriptive Statistics and Correlations of Three Measures of Multinationality for *Forbes'* The Most International U.S. Firms for the 1987-1992 Period

Panel A: Descriptive Statistics

	FP/TP[a]	FS/TS[b]	FA/TA[c]
Maximum	914.3	93	91
Third Quartile	61.9	47.4	41.4
Median	41.3	36.7	30.5
First Quartile	25	25.7	22.6
Minimum	0.2	6.6	2.7
Mean	52.81	37.45	39.92

Panel B: Correlations

	FP/TP	FS/TS	FA/TA
FP/TP	1.000		
FS/TS	0.280	1.000	
FA/TA	0.034	0.193*	1.000

*Denotes p-value < 0.05.
[a]FP/TP = Foreign profits/total profits
[b]FS/TS = Foreign sales/total sales
[c]FA/TA = Foreign assets/total assets

to-book equity (MQV), and the earnings/price ratio (EP). These variables are defined as follows:

$$MASS = [\text{Assets} - \text{Total Common Equity} + \text{Shares Outstanding} \times \text{Share Closing Price}]/\text{Assets}$$

$$MQV = [\text{Shares Outstanding} \times \text{Share Closing Price}]/\text{Total Common Equity}$$

$$EP = [\text{Primary EPS before Extraordinary Items}]/\text{Share Closing Price}$$

Descriptive statistics and correlation among the three measures of the investment opportunity set are presented in Exhibit 9.3. Correlations among the three variables are significant. The low correlations indicate that each variable makes a unique contribution as a measure of the in-

Exhibit 9.2

Selected Statistics Related to a Common Factor Analysis of Three Measures of Multinationality for *Forbes'* The Most International 100 U.S. Firms for the 1987-1992 Period

1. Eigenvalues of the Correlation Matrix

Eigenvalues	1	2	3
	1.3615	0.9680	0.6705

2. Factor Pattern

    FACTOR1

FS/TS	FP/TP	FA/TA
0.80529	0.50172	0.67918

3. Final Communality Estimates: Total = 1.361489

FS/TS	FP/TP	FA/TA
0.648491	0.251718	0.461280

4. Standardized Scoring Coefficients

    FACTOR1

FS/TS	FP/TP	FA/TA
0.59148	0.36850	0.49885

5. Descriptive Statistics of the Common Factor Extracted from the Three Measures of Multinationality

Maximum	2039.24
Third Quartile	74.70
Median	57.03
First Quartile	40.76
Minimum	5.17
Mean	64.35

Exhibit 9.3
Descriptive Statistics and Correlations of Three Measures of the
Investment Opportunity Set for *Forbes'* The Most International 100 U.S.
Firms for the 1987-1992 Period

Panel A: Descriptive Statistics

	MASS[a]	MQV[b]	EP[c]
Maximum	6.4943	60	0.5175
Third Quartile	1.8556	3.1851	0.1081
Median	1.2905	1.9090	0.0713
First Quartile	1.0618	1.2666	0.0482
Minimum	0.8745	0.3333	0.1536
Mean	0.3081	2.7020	0.0638

Panel B: Correlation

	MASS	MQV	EP
MASS	1.000		
MQV	0.0399*	1.000	
EP	0.0158*	0.0230*	1.000

*Denotes *p*-value < 0.05.
Variable Definitions
MASS = Market-to-book assets
MQV = Market-to-book equity
EP = Earnings/price ratio

vestment opportunity set. The results of the factor analysis are shown in Exhibit 9.4. One common factor appears to explain the interrelations among the three individual measures. Based on these factor scores, high-growth firms were chosen from the top 25 percent of the distribution factor scores while low-growth firms were chosen from the bottom 25 percent of the distribution factor scores.

Corporate Financing

The central corporate financing measure used in this study was a time series of the ratio of market debt to equity over the 1987–1992 period, computed as follows:

Exhibit 9.4
Selected Statistics Related to a Common Factor Analysis of Three Measures of the Investment Opportunity Set for *Forbes'* The Most International 100 U.S. Firms for the 1987-1992 Period

1.   Eigenvalues of the Correlation Matrix: Total = 3 Average = 1

Eigenvalue	1	2	3
	1.0540	0.9868	0.9592

2.   Factor Pattern

FACTOR1

MASS	MQV	EP
0.62821	0.66411	0.46722

3.   Final Communality Estimates: Total = 1.053994

MASS	MQV	EP
0.394651	0.441045	0.218299

4.   Standardized Scoring Coefficients

FACTOR1

MASS	MQV	EP
0.59603	0.63009	0.44329

5.   Descriptive Statistics of the Common Factor Extracted from the Three Measures of the Investment Opportunity

Maximum	9.3595
Third Quartile	3.2200
Median	2.0450
First Quartile	1.5085
Minimum	2.5209
Means	1.9812

Exhibit 9.5

Results of Overall Analysis of Covariance for Market Debt-to-Equity Ratio

Sources	F	P
Multinationality	13.62	0.0003
Investment Opportunity Set	88.06	0.0001
Interaction	10.34	0.0025
Covariates		
Size (Log of Assets)	69.21	0.0001
Annual Percentage Changes in GNP	0.08	0.7715
Annual Percentage Changes in Inflation	2.95	0.0875
Index of Business Formation	0.23	0.6337

Market Debt/Equity = Total Liabilities/[Shares Outstanding × Share Closing Price]

Covariates

Covariates included: the logarithm of total assets, annual percentage changes in gross national product and in inflation rate, and an index of net business formation. The logarithm of total assets was used to control for size. The other three covariates controlled for changes in corporate financing related to major shifts in aggregate demand. They also resulted in an analysis conditioned by macroeconomic variables. The macroeconomic variables were obtained from the *Economic Report of the President*.[23]

RESULTS

The effects on corporate financing of multinationality, the investment opportunity set, and their interaction are first examined by an *F*-test of the difference between variances after controlling for the covariates.

Exhibit 9.5 presents the results of the covariance analysis for market debt/equity. The overall analysis of covariance is statistically significant

Exhibit 9.6
Table of Means

Panel A: By Multinationality

Treatment	Mean	Standard Deviation	t-Probability
1. High Multinationality	11.6732	1.1741	0.0003
2. Low Multinationality	5.9107	1.0340	

Panel B: By Growth

Treatment	Mean	Standard Deviation	t-Probability
1. High Growth	6.3886	1.3492	0.0164
2. Low Growth	11.2153	1.1889	

$(F\ (7,200) = 4.30$, $p = 0.0002$, and $R^2 = 0.13)$. A further nondirectional F-test for differences in variance indicates that: (1) multinationality leads to a different capital structure, and (2) the investment opportunity set of the sample firms is associated with cross-sectional differences in capital structure. A third interesting result is the significant interaction effect, which implies the investment opportunity set has a different impact depending on the multinationality level. The significance level of the covariates indicates that only size and the annual percentage changes in inflation are important controls.

Exhibit 9.6 presents the results of the mean comparisons of the debt-to-equity ratio by growth type and multinationality type. **H1** states that growth firms have a lower debt-to-equity ratio than nongrowth firms. This is supported by the results in Exhibit 9.6, which show a significant difference between the debt/equity of high-growth firms (6.3886) and the debt/equity of low-growth firms (11.215). **H2** states that high-multinationality firms have a higher debt-to-equity ratio than low-multinationality firms. This is also supported by the results in Exhibit 9.6, which show a significant difference between the high-multinationality firms (11.6732) and the low-multinationality firms (5.9107).

Exhibit 9.7 presents the interaction effects of means. Exhibit 9.8 graphically illustrates that significant differences between the debt-to-equity ratio of high-growth firms and low-growth firms (as stated in **H1**)

Exhibit 9.7

Mean Comparisons of Market Debt-to-Equity Means of Multinationality and by Investment Opportunity Sets and *t*-Probabilities

Panel A: Means

Treatments	High Multinationality	Low Multinationality
1. High Investment Opportunity Set	7.9052	4.8320
2. Low Investment Opportunity Set	15.4411	6.9895

Panel B: t-Probability of Mean Comparisons

Treatments	1. Low Multinationality/ Low Investment Opportunity Set	2. Low Multinationality/ High Investment Opportunity Set	3. High Multinationality/ Low Investment Opportunity Set	4. High Multinationality/ High Investment Opportunity Set
1. Low Multinationality/ Low Investment Opportunity Set				
2. Low Multinationality/ High Investment Opportunity Set	0.0520			
3. High Multinationality/ Low Investment Opportunity Set	0.0001	0.0002		
4. High Multinationality/ High Investment Opportunity Set	0.0884	0.0870	0.0073	

hold under both high-multinationality and low-multinationality conditions, but at an increased level for high multinationality (as hypothesized in **H2**).

DISCUSSION

Our central proposition is that the investment opportunity set is associated with different capital structures in firms that have different levels of multinationality. The results support this contingency view of the relationship between the investment opportunity set and corporate financing.

Exhibit 9.8
Corporate Financing and Growth by Multinationality Type

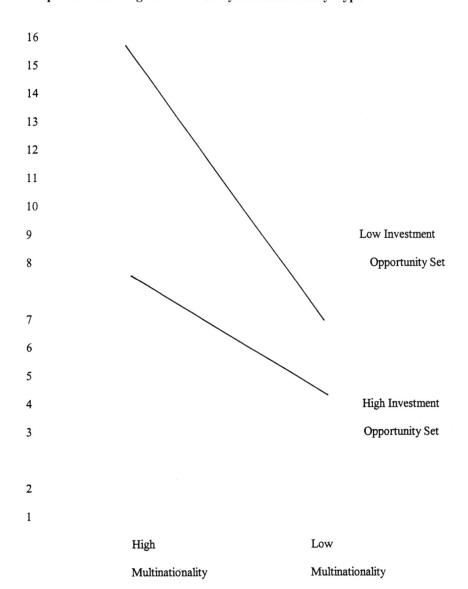

16
15
14
13
12
11
10
9   Low Investment
8   Opportunity Set
7
6
5
4   High Investment
3   Opportunity Set

2
1

High   Low

Multinationality   Multinationality

Hypothesis 1 was confirmed: growth firms have lower debt-to-equity ratios than nongrowth firms. Consistent with Smith and Watts[24] and Gaver and Gaver,[25] these results suggest that contracting cost explanations for corporate financing imply these decisions depend on the firm's investment opportunity set. Variation in the investment opportunity set leads to differences in the optimality of corporate financing with growth firms pursuing a lower debt-to-equity ratio than nongrowth firms.

Hypothesis 2 was confirmed: high-multinationality firms have higher debt/equity than low-multinationality firms. Multinational conditions call for more a debt-intensive capital structure.

The results also show a link between capital structure, the investment opportunity set, and multinationality. At different multinationality levels, different investment opportunity sets influence capital structure strategies.

These results complement and add to the strategic-group paradigm.[26] Based on a firm's heterogeneous capabilities and resources, the strategic-group paradigm enables researchers and practioners to consolidate industrial firms into sets of similar competitors, the so-called strategic groups. While a more comprehensive review of the literature is provided by McGee and Thomas,[27] Thomas and Venkatraman,[28] and Barney and Hoskisson,[29] the results of this study indicate that the strategic linkages between multinationality and the investment opportunity set need to be taken into account in the formation of strategic groups. Better strategic groups could be identified by a simultaneous consideration of multinationality and the investment opportunity set.

Additional research is needed to verify the results of this study and test questions that it raises. Replication needs to consider using different data and different measures of multinationality and investment opportunity set, as well as using a control group of essentially domestic firms. Until further research is completed, the results of the leverage differences must be interpreted with caution.

NOTES

1. F. Modigliani and M. H. Miller, "Corporate Income Taxes and the Cost of Capital: A Correction," *American Economic Review* 3 (1963): 433–443.

2. S. A. Ross, "The Determination of Financial Structure: The Incentive-Signaling Approach," *Bell Journal of Economics* 8 (1977): 23–40.

3. H. Leland and D. Pyle, "Informational Asymmetries, Financial Structure, and Financial Intermediation," *Journal of Finance* 32 (1977): 371–387.

4. M. Harris and A. Raviv, "Corporate Control Contests and Capital Structure," *Journal of Financial Economics* 20 (1988): 55–86.

5. M. C. Jensen and W. H. Meckling, "Theory of the Firm: Managerial Behavior Agency Costs and Ownership Structure," *Journal of Financial Economics* 3 (1976): 305–360.

6. S. C. Myers, "Determinants of Corporate Borrowing," *Journal of Financial Economics* 5 (1977): 147–176.

7. M. C. Jensen, "Agency Costs of Free Cash Flow, Corporate Finance, and Takeovers," *American Economic Review* 76 (1986): 323–329.

8. S. C. Myers, "The Capital Structure Puzzle," *Journal of Finance* 39 (1984): 575–591.

9. These theories suggest that the firm's choice of capital structure is a function of attributes that determine the various costs and benefits associated with debt and equity financing (Titman and Wessels, 1988). These attributes include the collateral value of assets (Scott, 1977; Myers and Majluf, 1984); nondebt tax shields (DeAngelo and Masulis, 1980); growth (Jensen and Meckling, 1976; Warner, 1977; Green, 1984); uniqueness (Titman, 1984); firm size (Warner, 1977; Ang et al., 1982); industry classification (Belkaoui, 1975; Titman, 1984); volatility (Titman and Wessels, 1988); and profitability (Donaldson, 1961; Brealy and Myers, 1984).

10. S. L. Barton and P. J. Gordon, "Corporate Strategy: Useful Perspective for the Study of Capital Structure?" *Academy of Management Review* 12 (1987): 67–75.

11. A similar strategy perspective has been implied by several financial theorists who are (1) frustrated by the lack of understanding of the issue (Myers, 1984, p. 575), or by the "absurd" results that some theories may imply (Ross, 1977), and (2) interested in the exploration of behavior beyond what is allowed by mathematical modeling (Hempel, 1983), interested in the role of top management in the capital structure decision (Donaldson, 1961, p. 87; Carleton, 1978; Walker and Petty, 1978; Andrews, 1980), or concerned that multiple objectives and contextual factors that are not financial in nature may be important to the problem (Findlay and Whitmore, 1974; Carleton and Silberman, 1977).

12. Myers, "Determinants of Corporate Borrowing," 147–176.

13. J. J. Gaver and K. M. Gaver, "Additional Evidence on the Association between the Investment Opportunity Set and Corporate Financing Dividend, and Compensation Policies," *Journal of Accounting and Economics* 16 (1993): 125–160.

14. C. W. Smith and R. L. Watts, "The Investment Opportunity Set and Corporate Financing, Dividend and Compensation Policies," *Journal of Financial Economics* 32 (1992): 263–292.

15. Jeff Madura, *International Financial Management* (St. Paul, MN: West Publishing Company, 1995).

16. Ibid.

17. John H. Dunning, "Reappraising the Eclectic Paradigm in an Age of Alliance Capitalism," *Journal of International Business Studies* 26 (1995): 461–492.

18. John M. Stopford and Louis T. Wells, *Managing the Multinational Enterprise* (New York: Basic Books, 1972).

19. Howard V. Perlmutter, "The Tortuous Evaluation of the Multinational Corporation," *Columbia Journal of World Business* 4 (January-February 1969): 9–18.

20. D. Sullivan, "Measuring the Degree of Internationalization of a Firm," *Journal of International Business Studies* 25 (1994): 325–342.

21. Smith and Watts, "The Investment Opportunity Set and Corporate Financing, Dividend and Compensation Policies," 263–292.

22. Gaver and Gaver, "Additional Evidence on the Association between the Investment Opportunity Set and Corporate Financing Dividend, and Compensation Policies," 125–160.

23. *Economic Report of the President* (Washington, DC: U.S. Government Printing Office, 1995).

24. Smith and Watts, "The Investment Opportunity Set and Corporate Financing, Dividend and Compensation Policies," 263–292.

25. Gaver and Gaver, "Additional Evidence on the Association between the Investment Opportunity Set and Corporate Financing Dividend, and Compensation Policies," 125–160.

26. M. Porter, *Competitive Advantage: Creating and Sustaining Superior Performance* (New York: Free Press, 1985).

27. J. McGee and H. Thomas, "Strategic Groups: Theory, Research and Taxonomy," *Strategic Management Journal* 7 (1986): 141–160.

28. H. Thomas and N. Venkatraman, "Research on Strategic Groups: Progress and Prognosis," *Journal of Management Studies* 25 (1988): 537–555.

29. J. B. Barney and R. E. Hoskisson, "Untested Assertions in Strategic Group Research," *Managerial and Decision Economics* 11 (1990): 187–198.

SELECTED READINGS

Andrews, K. R. *The Concept of Corporate Strategy*. Homewood, IL: Irwin, 1980.

Ang, J., J. Chua, and J. McConnell. "The Administrative Costs of Corporate Bankruptcy: A Note." *Journal of Finance* 37 (1982): 219–226.

Barney, J. B., and R. E. Hoskisson. "Untested Assertions in Strategic Group Research." *Managerial and Decision Economics* 11 (1990): 187–198.

Barton, S. L., and P. J. Gordon. "Corporate Strategy: Useful Perspective for the Study of Capital Structure?" *Academy of Management Review* 12 (1987): 67–75.

Belkaoui, A., "A Canadian Survey of Financial Structure." *Financial Management* 4 (1975): 74–79.

Brealy, R., and S. Myers. *Principles of Corporate Finance.* New York: McGraw-Hill, 1984.

Carleton, W. T. "An Agenda for More Effective Research in Corporate Finance." *Financial Management* 4 (1978): 79.

Carleton, W. T., and I. H. Silberman. "Joint Determination of Rate of Return and Capital Structure: An Economic Analysis." *Journal of Finance* 32 (1977): 811–821.

DeAngelo, H., and R. Masulis. "Optimal Capital Structure under Corporate and Personal Taxation." *Journal of Financial Economics* 8 (1980): 3–27.

Donaldson, G. *Corporate Debt Capacity: A Study of Corporate Debt Policy and the Determinants of Corporate Debt Capacity.* Boston: Harvard University Graduate School of Business, Division of Research, 1961.

Dunning, John H. "Reappraising the Eclectic Paradigm in an Age of Alliance Capitalism." *Journal of International Business Studies* 26 (1995): 461–492.

Economic Report of the President (Washington, DC: U.S. Government Printing Office, 1995.

Findlay, M. C., and G. A. Whitmore. "Beyond Shareholder Wealth Maximization." *Financial Management* 4 (1974): 25–35.

Gaver, J. J. and K. M. Gaver. "Additional Evidence on the Association between the Investment Opportunity Set and Corporate Financing Dividend, and Compensation Policies." *Journal of Accounting and Economics* 16 (1993): 125–160.

Green, R. "Investment Incentives, Debt, and Warrants." *Journal of Financial Economics* 12 (1984): 115–135.

Harris, M., and A. Raviv. "Corporate Control Contests and Capital Structure." *Journal of Financial Economics* 20 (1988): 55–86.

Hempel, G. H. "Teaching and Research in Finance: Perceptions, Conflicts, and the Future." *Financial Management* 12 (1983): 5–10.

Jensen, M. C. "Agency Costs of Free Cash Flow, Corporate Finance, and Takeovers." *American Economic Review* 76 (1986): 323–329.

Jensen, M. C. and W. H. Meckling. "Theory of the Firm: Managerial Behavior Agency Costs and Ownership Structure." *Journal of Financial Economics* 3 (1976): 305–360.

Leland, H., and D. Pyle. "Information Asymmetries, Financial Structure, and Financial Intermediation." *Journal of Finance* 32 (1977): 371–387.

Madura, Jeff. *International Financial Management.* St. Paul, MN: West Publishing Company, 1995.

McGee, J., and H. Thomas. "Strategic Groups: Theory, Research and Taxonomy." *Strategic Management Journal* 7 (1986): 141–160.

Modigliani, F., and M. H. Miller. "Corporate Income Taxes and the Cost of Capital: A Correction." *American Economic Review* 3 (1963): 433–443.

Montgomery, C. A., and H. Singh. "Diversification Strategy and Systematic Risk." *Strategic Management Journal* 5 (1984): 181–191.

Myers, S. C. "Determinants of Corporate Borrowing." *Journal of Financial Economics* 5 (1977): 147–176.

———. "The Capital Structure Puzzle." *Journal of Finance* 39 (1984): 575–591.

Myers, S. C., and N. Majluf. "Corporate Financing and Investment Decisions When Firms Have Information Investors Do Not Have." *Journal of Financial Economics* 13 (1984): 187–221.

Perlmutter, Howard V. "The Tortuous Evaluation of the Multinational Corporation." *Columbia Journal of World Business* 4 (January-February 1969): 9–18.

Porter, M. *Competitive Advantage: Creating and Sustaining Superior Performance*. New York: Free Press, 1985.

Ross, S. A. "The Determination of Financial Structure: The Incentive-Signaling Approach." *Bell Journal of Economics* 8 (1977): 23–40.

Scott, J. "Bankruptcy, Secured Debt, and Optimal Capital Structure." *Journal of Finance* 32 (1977): 1–19.

Smith, C. W., and R. L. Watts. "The Investment Opportunity Set and Corporate Financing, Dividend and Compensation Policies." *Journal of Financial Economics* 32 (1992): 263–292.

Stopford, John M., and Louis T. Wells. *Managing the Multinational Enterprise*. New York: Basic Books, 1972.

Sullivan, D. "Measuring the Degree of Internationalization of a Firm." *Journal of International Business Studies* 25 (1994): 325–342.

Thomas, H., and N. Venkatraman. "Research on Strategic Groups: Progress and Prognosis." *Journal of Management Studies* 25 (1988): 537–555.

Titman, S. "The Effect of Capital Structure on a Firm's Liquidation Decision." *Journal of Financial Economics* 13 (1984): 137–151.

Titman, S., and R. Wessels. "The Determinants of Capital Structure Choice." *Journal of Finance* 43 (1988): 1–19.

Walker, E. W., and J. W. Petty. "Financial Differences between Large and Small Firms." *Financial Management* 4 (1978): 61–68.

Warner, J. "Bankruptcy Costs: Some Evidence." *Journal of Finance* 32 (1977): 337–347.

10

Determinants of Prediction Performance of Earnings Forecasts Internationally: The Effects of Disclosure, Economic Risk, and Alignment of Financial and Tax Accounting

INTRODUCTION

With the gradual growth and integration of global financial markets, financial analysts' accurate provisions of earnings forecasts, buy/sell recommendations, and other information to brokers, money managers, and institutional investors are acquiring international importance. Analysis and/or comparison of analysts' forecasts internationally show marked differences in the prediction performance of earnings forecasts internationally.[1-10] Determining the variables causing these differences is important to those users who rely on the earnings forecasts for their resource allocation decisions, and to policymakers in each country affected who need to improve the accuracy of earnings forecasts. Accordingly, this study considered whether disclosure policy, level of economic risk, and level of alignment of financial and tax accounting explain differences in financial analysts' forecast (FAF) error internationally. The results on fourteen countries for the 1992–1994 period suggest that levels of FAF error are negatively related to the level of disclosure requirements of global stock exchanges and positively related to the levels of economic risk and alignment of financial and tax accounting.

BACKGROUND AND HYPOTHESIS

The study proposes three determinants of prediction performance of earnings forecasts internationally—disclosure policy, economic risk, and level of alignment of financial and tax accounting.

Disclosure Policy

The empirical evidence is consistent with the notion that the General Agreement on Tariffs and Trade (GATT) rules in each country reflect the specific and unique set of institutional features relevant to each country.[11,12] Among the institutional differences advanced by Riahi-Belkaoui,[13] Edwards,[14] Jacobson and Aaker,[15] and Falk[16] are those relating to political structures, linguistic and cultural affiliation, tax structures, intercorporate ownership, industrial relations, type of economic system, and economic, social, and religious policies. The end result is that the level of disclosure in general and the mandated disclosures by stock exchanges in particular will differ.[17] The differences in the disclosure levels mandated by stock exchanges lead to a difference in the level of informativeness about future earnings, a situation likely to affect the accuracy of analysts' earnings forecasts. This leads to the following hypothesis:

H1: The financial analysts' forecast error is negatively associated with the level of disclosure requirements of stock exchanges.

Economic Risk

Economic risk arises from instability in economic factors. It is manifest in higher inflation and debt servicing costs.[18] The likely relationship between economic risk and forecast accuracy is straightforward. To the extent that instability in economic factors is not very informative about future earnings, analysts' forecast accuracy will decrease with the low informativeness created by economic risk. Given that the instability in economic factors is definitively not useful to analysts, it is not difficult to imagine scenarios in which an increase in economic risk in a given country systematically reduces the accuracy of analysts' earnings forecasts. The strength of the relationship between economic risk and financial analysts' forecast error is, however, an empirical one. This leads to the following hypothesis:

H2: The financial analysts' forecast error is positively associated with the level of the country's economic risk.

Alignment of Financial and Tax Accounting

A major variable differentiating the level of disclosure between countries is the important role played by tax rules in the production of financial statements. Generally labeled as tax relativism, it implies that the level of alignment between financial and tax accounting determines the level of disclosure in each country. The difference between the level of conformity between financial and tax accounting raises a question about the value relevance of financial data in high-alignment countries.[19-21] High-alignment countries are more likely to be associated with concentrated ownership,[22] with owners likely to have access to the information before its publication,[23] and more likely to have creditor orientation and to put more emphasis on valuing balance sheets.[24] In addition, firms in high-alignment countries have more incentives to manipulate income downward to minimize taxes.[25,26] All of the above arguments contribute further toward decreasing the value-relevance of financial data used by financial analysts in the determination of financial forecasts. The strength of the relation between the level of alignment of financial and tax accounting and financial analysts' forecast error needs, however, to be tested. This leads to the following hypothesis:

H3: The financial analysts' forecast error is positively associated with the level of alignment of financial and tax accounting.

EMPIRICAL ANALYSIS

Sample

Countries were selected on the basis of available data from the 1994 domestic and international Institutional Brokers Estimate System (I/B/E/S) tapes. Countries and firms (in parentheses) included in the analysis were: Australia (50), Canada (97), Denmark (60), France (60), Germany (60), Italy (60), Japan (183), the Netherlands (60), Spain (60), Switzerland (60), United Kingdom (125), and United States (450). The number and choice of firms were motivated by the following criteria: (a) The number of firms for each country reflects the capital market size with a higher number allocated to countries with large capital market size, and (b) the firms included had available and valid data for the analysis, and more than two analysts making earnings forecasts.

Financial Analysts' Forecast Error

The financial analysts' predictions of annual earnings for the firms of each country in the sample and the actual earnings reported by the firms were used to determine the dependent variable: the average mean squared forecast error (MS). It is used as a measure of the forecast error. Reference for this measure is based on its mathematical and statistical tractability and the more than proportional weight given to large error, a desirable assumption in economic forecasting.[27] It is defined as follows:

$$MS = 1/N \sum_{J=1}^{N} (Pj - Rj)^2$$

where:

$j =$ firm,
$Pj = Fjt - Ajt$
$Rj = Ajt - Ajt - 1$

Fjt is the current forecast for firm j at time t. Ajt is the current period's earnings. $Ajt-1$ is the prior period's earnings. N is the number of observations.

Economic Risk

The study relies on the risk rating scores provided by the International Country Risk Guide (ICRG) of International Business Communication Ltd.[28] ICRG receives the most attention from foreign investors.[29] ICRG provides a composite risk rating, as well as individual ratings for political, financial, and economic risk. The interest in this study is with the economic component, which is economic risk. This economic component includes such factors as inflation and debt service costs.[30] The maximum or least risky score is 50 for economic risk. It is shown in Exhibit 10.1 for each of the countries used in the sample.

Exhibit 10.1
Sample Description

Country	Alignment of Financial and Tax Accounting	Economic Risk	Disclosure Score
1. *Australia*	low level	37.0	74.60
2. *Canada*	low level	37.0	79.00
3. *Denmark*	low level	37.0	67.20
4. *France*	high level	34.5	76.20
5. *Germany*	high level	38.5	67.20
6. *Italy*	high level	25.0	68.46
7. *Japan*	high level	39.0	77.68
8. *Korea*	high level	36.5	71.43
9. *Netherlands*	low level	40.5	73.19
10. *South Africa*	low level	37.5	74.50
11. *Spain*	high level	35.0	68.84
12. *Switzerland*	high level	39.5	52.24
13. *United Kingdom*	low level	36.0	86.21
14. *U.S.A*	low level	39.5	90.31

Alignment of Financial and Tax Accounting

The fourteen countries used in the analysis were classified as having either low or high alignment between financial and tax accounting (see Exhibit 10.1). The section on "book and tax differences" from the series of Price Waterhouse publications in business environment in different countries was used as the primary source of the classification. High-level countries were coded 1, and low-level countries were coded 0.

Adhikari and Tondkar's Disclosure Index

Adhikari and Tondkar's composite disclosure index,[31] intended to measure the quantity and intensity of disclosure required as part of the listing and filing requirements of stock exchanges, includes a list of forty-four items. An actual score for each stock exchange was obtained by

Adhikari and Tondkar by summing all the scores received by the stock exchanges for the forty-four information items that are required by the stock exchange as part of its listing and filing requirements. The disclosure score was obtained by dividing the actual score attained by a stock exchange by the maximum attainable score. To account for differences among different user groups, each disclosure score was weighted by its relevance to a list of experts from each of the countries examined. As a result, a weighted score (WTDSCORE) was computed. They are shown in Exhibit 10.1. The index, as based on 1989 data, reflects a disclosure culture assumed to be rigid and slow to change, justifying its use to analyze 1994 analysts' errors.

Procedures

Cross-sectional regressions are run between the average mean squared forecast error of each country on one hand and the corresponding level of disclosure requirements of stock exchanges, economic risk, and level of alignment of financial and tax accounting on the other hand. The model is as follows:

$$MS_t = A_{t0} + A_{t1}WTDSCORE_t + A_{t2}ER + A_{t3}LOA_t$$

where:

$$MS_t = \text{Average mean square forecast error}$$
$$WTDSCORE_t = \text{Weighted disclosure score}$$
$$ER = \text{Economic risk}$$
$$LOA = \text{Level of alignment of financial and tax accounting}$$

RESULTS

The three hypotheses state that the financial analysts' forecast error internationally is related negatively to the level of disclosure requirements of stock exchanges and positively to the level of economic risk and the level of alignment of financial and tax accounting.

Exhibit 10.2 presents the results of the regression analysis. As the F-statistic indicates, the general regression is significant with the three independent variables explaining 63.59 percent of the financial analysts'

Exhibit 10.2
Multiple Regression of MS_t on Disclosure Score, Economic Risk, and Level of Alignment[1]

$$MS_t^2 = A_{t0} + A_{t1} \, WTDSCORE + A_{t2} \, ER + A_{t3} \, LOA + R$$

Years	A_{t0}	A_{t1}	A_{t2}	A_{t3}	F	R2 Adjusted
1992-94	-0.0229 (0.213)	-0.0810 (4.291)*	0.1596 4.168*	0.0608 2.254**	8.569*	63.59%

[1]t-statistics are in parentheses.
*Significant at $\alpha = 0.01$.
**Significant at $\alpha = 0.05$.
Variable Definitions
MS_t = Average mean square forecast error
$WTDSCORE$ = Weighted disclosure score
ER = Economic risk
LOA = Level of alignment of financial and tax accounting

forecast error. The level of disclosure requirements of stock exchanges was significant in the exact direction to the stated hypothesis **H1**. In other words, the results show that the higher the level of disclosure requirements for stock exchanges, the lower the financial analysts' forecast error. They show that the level of disclosure requirements of a stock exchange, as an expression of the informativeness of each country's disclosure policy, increases the accuracy of analysts' earnings forecasts. This result is in conformity with U.S.-based findings on how disclosure affects favorably analysts' forecasts.[32–39]

Economic risk was significant in the exact direction to the stated hypothesis **H2**. In other words, the results show that the higher the level of economic risk, the higher the financial analysts' forecast error internationally. They indicate that, in economically risky situations, the financial analysts deal with more uncertainties and have a more complex environment for the forecasting of earnings, which reduce their forecasting abilities and yield a higher forecast error.

The level of alignment of financial and tax accounting was significant in the exact direction of the stated hypothesis **H3**. In other words, the results show that the higher the level of alignment of financial and tax accounting, the higher the level of financial analysts' forecast error. This is in conformity with the thesis that firms in high-alignment countries have the incentive to manipulate income downward to minimize taxes, contributing further toward decreasing the value-relevance of financial data used by financial analysts in the determination of earnings forecasts.[40,41]

CONCLUSIONS

The results of this chapter indicate that the level of financial analysts' forecast error (FAF) internationally is negatively related to the level of disclosure requirements of global stock exchanges, and positively related to the levels of economic risk and alignment of financial and tax accounting. The results are consistent with earlier studies in the U.S. context with the view that more forthcoming disclosure policies lead to more accurate forecasts. They are also consistent with the established thesis connecting economic risk and alignment of financial and tax accounting with reduced relevance of financial accounting data, leading also to less accurate forecasts. To the extent that the behavior of analysts internationally captures the disclosure policy and the levels of economic risk and alignment of financial and tax accounting, these results have implications for users of international forecasts and standards setters in each country as they set disclosure policy. Users of financial analysts' forecasts should put more weight on the forecasts originating from countries with a high level of disclosure, a low level of economic risk, and a low level of alignment of financial and tax accounting. Standard setters in each country need to set a higher level of disclosure policy and reduce the alignment of financial and tax accounting in order to increase the relevance of accounting data and reduce the level of forecast error.

NOTES

1. Vivek Mande, "A Comparison of U.S. and Japanese Analysts' Forecasts of Earnings and Sales," *International Journal of Accounting* 31 (1996): 143–160.

2. John Capstaff, Krishan Paudyal, and William Rees, "The Accuracy and Rationality of Earnings Forecasts by U.K. Analysts," *Journal of Business Finance and Accounting* 22, no. 1 (1995): 67–85.

3. J. Arnold and P. Moizer, "A Survey of the Methods Used by U.K. Investments Analysts to Appraise Investments in Ordinary Shares," *Accounting and Business Research* 14 (1984): 195–207.

4. J. M. Rivera, "Prediction Performance of Earnings Forecasts: The Case of U.S. Multinationals," *Journal of International Business Studies* 22, no. 12 (1991): 915–921.

5. Ahmed Riahi-Belkaoui, "Prediction Performance of Earnings Forecasts

of U.S. Firms Active in Developed and Developing Countries," *Advances in Accounting in Emerging Economies* 3 (1995): 85–97.

6. J. O'Hanlon and R. Whiddett, "Do U.K. Security Analysts Overact?" *Accounting and Business Research* 22 (1991): 63–74.

7. D. H. Patz, "U.K. Analysts' Earnings Forecasts," *Accounting and Business Research* 19 (1985): 267–275.

8. R. Rike, J. Meeyanssen, and L. Chadwick, "The Appraisal of Ordinary Shares by Investment Analysts in the U.K and Germany," *Accounting and Business Research* 24 (1993): 489–499.

9. J. Y. Cho, "Properties of Market Expectations of Accounting Earnings by Financial Analysts: U.K. versus U.S.," *Accounting and Business Research* 24 (1994): 230–240.

10. Somnath Das and S. M. Saudagaran, "Properties of Analysts' Earnings Forecasts for Cross-Listed Foreign Firms," *Contemporary Accounting Research* (Forthcoming.)

11. Helen Gernon and R. S. Olusegum Wallace, "International Accounting Research: A Review of Its Ecology, Contending Theories and Methodologies," *Journal of Accounting Literature* 14 (1995): 54–106.

12. R. S. O. Wallace and Helen Gernon, "Frameworks for International Comparative Financial Accounting," *Journal of Accounting Literature* 10 (1991): 209–264.

13. Ahmed Riahi-Belkaoui, *International and Multinational Accounting* (London: Dryden Press, 1994).

14. F. Edwards, "Listing of Foreign Securities on U.S. Exchanges," *Journal of Applied Corporate Finance* 5 (1993): 28–36.

15. R. Jacobson and D. Aaker, "Myopic Management Behavior with Efficient, but Imperfect, Financial Markets: A Comparison of Information Asymmetries in the U.S. and Japan," *Journal of Accounting and Economics* 16 (1993): 383–405.

16. H. Falk, "International Accounting: A Quest for Research," *Contemporary Accounting Research* 11 (1994): 595–615.

17. A. Adhikari and R. H. Tondkar, "Environmental Factors Influencing Accounting Disclosure Requirements of Global Stock Exchanges," *Journal of International Financial Management and Accounting* 4 (1992): 76–105.

18. M. Janah, "Rating Risk in Hot Countries," *Wall Street Journal* (September 20, 1991): R4.

19. P. Joos and M. Lang, "The Effects of Accounting Diversity: Evidence from the European Union," *Journal of Accounting Research* 32, Supplement (1994): 141–176.

20. M. Harris and A. Raviv, "Differences in Opinion Make a Horse Race," *Review of Financial Studies* 6 (1993): 473–494.

21. A. Alford, J. Jones, R. Leftwich, and M. Zmigewski, "Relative Inform-

ativeness of Accounting Disclosures in Different Countries," *Journal of Accounting Research* 31 (1993): 183–223.

22. G. G. Muller, H. Gernon, and G. Meek, *Accounting and International Perspective* (New York: Business One Irwin, 1994).

23. Ali Ashiq and Lee-Seok Hwang, "The Effect of Alignment of Financial and Tax Accounting on the Value Relevance of Financial Accounting Data: Evidence from Cross-Country Comparison," Working Paper, University of Arizona (July 1996).

24. S. J. Gray, L. G. Campbell, and J. C. Shaw, *International Financial Reporting: A Comparative International Survey of Accounting Requirements and Practices in 30 Countries* (London: Macmillan Publishers Limited, 1984).

25. Joos and Lang, "The Effects of Accounting Diversity: Evidence from the European Union," 141–176.

26. Alford, Jones, Leftwich, and Zmigewski, "Relative Informativeness of Accounting Disclosures in Different Countries," 183–223.

27. H. Theil, *Applied Economic Forecasting* (Amsterdam: North-Holland Publishing Company, 1966).

28. Janah, "Rating Risk in Hot Countries," R4.

29. S. H. Kim and S. H. Kim, *Global Corporate Finance: Text and Cases*, 2d ed. (Miami: Kolb Publishing, 1993).

30. Janah, "Rating Risk in Hot Countries," R4.

31. Adhikari and Tondkar, "Environmental Factors Influencing Accounting Disclosure Requirements of Global Stock Exchanges," 76–105.

32. S. Baginski and J. Hassell, "The Market Interpretation of Management Earnings Forecasts as a Predictor of Subsequent Financial Analyst Forecast Revision," *Accounting Review* 65 (January 1990): 175–190.

33. R. Jennings, "Unsystematic Security Price Movements, Managerial Earnings Forecasts, and Revisions in Consensus Analysts Earning Forecasts," *Journal of Accounting Research* 25 (Spring 1987): 90–110.

34. G. Waymire, "Additional Evidence on the Accuracy of Analyst Forecasts before and after Voluntary Management Earnings Forecasts," *Accounting Review* 59 (January 1986): 129–142.

35. L. Brown and J. Han, "The Impact of Annual Earning Announcements on Convergence of Beliefs," *Accounting Review* 67 (October 1992): 862–875.

36. S. Swaminathan, "The Impact of SEC Mandated Segment Data on Price Variability and Divergence of Beliefs," *Accounting Review* 66 (January 1991): 23–41.

37. B. Baldwin, "Segment Earnings Disclosure and the Ability of Security Analysts to Forecast Earnings per Share," *Accounting Review* 59 (July 1984): 376–389.

38. L. Brown and M. Rozeff, "The Predictive Value of Interim Reports for Improving Forecasts of Future Quarterly Earnings," *Accounting Review* 56 (July 1979): 585–591.

39. Mark H. Lang and R. J. Lundholm, "Corporate Disclosure Policy and Analyst Behavior," *Accounting Review* 4 (October 1996): 467–492.

40. Joos and Lang, "The Effects of Accounting Diversity," 141–176.

41. Alford, Jones, Leftwich, and Zmigewski, "Relative Informativeness of Accounting Disclosures in Different Countries," 183–223.

SELECTED READINGS

Adhikari, A., and R. H. Tondkar. "Environmental Factors Influencing Accounting Disclosure Requirements of Global Stock Exchanges." *Journal of International Financial Management and Accounting* 4 (1992): 76–105.

Alford, A., J. Jones, R. Leftwich, and M. Zmigewski. "Relative Informativeness of Accounting Disclosures in Different Countries." *Journal of Accounting Research* 31 (1993): 183–223.

Arnold, J., and P. Moizer. "A Survey of the Methods Used by U.K. Investment Analysts to Appraise Investments in Ordinary Shares." *Accounting and Business Research* 14 (1984): 195–207.

Ashiq, Ali, and Lee-Seok Hwang. "The Effect of Alignment of Financial and Tax Accounting on the Value Relevance of Financial Accounting Data: Evidence from Cross-Country Comparison." Working Paper, University of Arizona, July 1996.

Baginski, S., and J. Hassell. "The Market Interpretation of Management Earnings Forecasts as a Predictor of Subsequent Financial Analyst Forecast Revision." *Accounting Review* 65 (January 1990): 175–190.

Baldwin, B. "Segment Earnings Disclosure and the Ability of Security Analysts to Forecast Earnings Per Share." *Accounting Review* 59 (July 1984): 376–389.

Brown, L., and J. Han. "The Impact of Annual Earning Announcements on Convergence of Beliefs." *Accounting Review* 67 (October 1992): 862–875.

Brown, L., and M. Rozeff. "The Predictive Value of Interim Reports for Improving Forecasts of Future Quarterly Earnings." *Accounting Review* 56 (July 1979): 585–591.

Capstaff, John, Krishan Paudyal, and William Rees. "The Accuracy and Rationality of Earnings Forecasts by U.K. Analysts." *Journal of Business Finance and Accounting* 22, no. 1 (1995): 67–85.

Cho, J. Y. "Properties of Market Expectations of Accounting Earnings by Financial Analysts: U.K. versus U.S." *Accounting and Business Research* 24 (1994): 230–240.

Das, Somnath, and S. M. Saudagaran. "Properties of Analysts' Earnings Forecasts for Cross-Listed Foreign Firms." *Contemporary Accounting Research* (Forthcoming).

Edwards, F. "Listing of Foreign Securities on U.S. Exchanges." *Journal of Applied Corporate Finance* 5 (1993): 28–36.

Falk, H. "International Accounting: A Quest for Research." *Contemporary Accounting Research* 11 (1994): 595–615.

Gernon, Helen, and R. S. Olusegum Wallace. "International Accounting Research: A Review of Its Ecology, Contending Theories and Methodologies." *Journal of Accounting Literature* 14 (1995): 54–106.

Gray, S. J., L. G. Campbell, and J. C. Shaw. *International Financial Reporting: A Comparative International Survey of Accounting Requirements and Practices in 30 Countries.* London: Macmillan Publishers Limited, 1984.

Harris, M., and A. Raviv. "Differences in Opinion Make a Horse Race." *Review of Financial Studies* 6 (1993): 473–494.

Jacobson, R., and D. Aaker. "Myopic Management Behavior with Efficient, but Imperfect, Financial Markets: A Comparison of Information Asymmetries in the U.S. and Japan." *Journal of Accounting and Economics* 16 (1993): 383–405.

Janah, M. "Rating Risk in Hot Countries." *Wall Street Journal* (September 20, 1991): R4.

Jennings, R. "Unsystematic Security Price Movements, Managerial Earnings Forecasts, and Revisions in Consensus Analysts Earnings Forecasts." *Journal of Accounting Research* 25 (Spring 1987): 90–110.

Joos, P., and M. Lang. "The Effects of Accounting Diversity: Evidence from the European Union." *Journal of Accounting Research* 32, Supplement (1994): 141–176.

Kim, S. H., and S. H. Kim. *Global Corporate Finance: Text and Cases*, 2d ed. Miami: Kolb Publishing, 1993.

Lang, Mark H., and R. J. Lundholm. "Corporate Disclosure Policy and Analyst Behavior." *Accounting Review* 4 (October 1996): 467–492.

Mande, Vivek. "A Comparison of U.S. and Japanese Analysts' Forecasts of Earnings and Sales." *International Journal of Accounting* 31 (1996): 143–160.

Muller, G. G., H. Gernon, and G. Meek. *Accounting and International Perspective.* New York: Business One Irwin, 1994.

O'Hanlon, J., and R. Whiddett. "Do U.K. Security Analysts Overact?" *Accounting and Business Research* 22 (1991): 63–74.

Patz, D. H. "U.K. Analysts' Earnings Forecasts." *Accounting and Business Research* 19 (1985): 267–275.

Riahi-Belkaoui, Ahmed. *International and Multinational Accounting.* London: Dryden Press, 1994.

———. "Prediction Performance of Earnings Forecast of U.S. Firms Active in Developed And Developing Countries." *Advances in Accounting in Emerging Economies* 3 (1995): 85–97.

Rike, R., J. Meeyanssen, and L. Chadwick. "The Appraisal of Ordinary Shares by Investment Analysts in the U.K. and Germany.''*Accounting and Business Research* 24 (1993): 489–499.

Rivera, J. M. ''Prediction Performance of Earnings Forecasts: The Case of U.S. Multinationals.'' *Journal of International Business Studies* 22, no. 112, (1991).

Swaminathan, S. ''The Impact of SEC Mandated Segment Data on Price Variability and Divergence of Beliefs.'' *Accounting Review* 66 (January 1991): 23–41.

Theil, H. *Applied Economic Forecasting.* Amsterdam: North-Holland Publishing Company, 1966.

Wallace, R. S. O., and Helen Gernon. ''Frameworks for International Comparative Financial Accounting.'' *Journal of Accounting Literature* 10 (1991): 209–264.

Waymire, G. ''Additional Evidence on the Accuracy of Analyst Forecasts before and after Voluntary Management Earnings Forecasts.''*Accounting Review* 59 (January 1986): 129–142.

Empirical Validation of a General Model of Growth Opportunities

INTRODUCTION

The firm is comprised of values assets-in-place and future investment options or growth opportunities. The lower the proportion of firm value represented by assets-in-place, the higher the growth opportunities. Myers describes these potential investment opportunities as call options whose values depend on the likelihood that management will exercise them.[1] Like call options, these growth opportunities represent real value to the firm.[2] Growth options include such discretionary expenditures as capacity expansion projects, new product introductions, acquisition of other firms, investments in brand name through advertising, and even maintenance and replacement of existing assets.[3] A significant portion of the market value of equity is accounted for by growth opportunities.[4-6] In addition, empirical results suggest that growth opportunities influence various corporate policy decisions.[7-12] In light of the importance of growth opportunities, this study states first a general model of growth opportunities that can be used to estimate growth opportunities. Second, empirical evidence is provided to validate this statement.

Exhibit 11.1
A General Model of Growth Opportunities

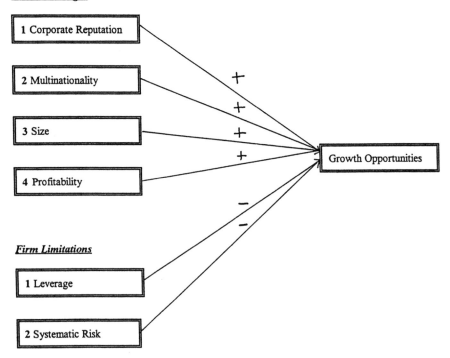

A GENERAL MODEL OF GROWTH OPPORTUNITIES

A general and operationally testable model of growth opportunities rests on combining the firm advantages and limitations. As shown in Exhibit 11.1, the model argues that growth opportunities, as measured by the investment opportunity set, are positively related to the firm advantages of corporate reputation, multinationality, size, and profitability, and negatively related to leverage and systematic risk.

The rationale for the model follows.

Reputation Advantages

The reputation of a firm is crucial for various decisions ranging from resource allocation and career decisions to production choices, to name only a few.[13] It is an important signal of the firms' organizational effectiveness.[14] To create the right impression or reputation, firms signal their key characteristics to constituents to maximize their social status.[15] In fact, corporate audiences were found to construct reputations on the basis of accounting and market information or signals regarding firm performance.[16–18] These reputations have become established and constitute signals that may affect the actions of firms' stakeholders. Specifically, a good reputation can be construed as a competitive advantage within an industry.[19] Favorable reputations can create favorable situations for firms that include: (1) the generation of excess returns by inhibiting the mobility of rivals in an industry[20]; (2) the capability of charging premium prices to consumers[21]; and (3) the creation of a better image in the capital markets and to investors.[22] Those situations create growth opportunities for the firm. Accordingly the following hypothesis applies:

H1: Growth opportunities, as measured by the investment opportunity set, vary directly with the level of reputation.

Multinationality Advantages

The multinational firm is a collection of valuable options and generates profits that enhance its value.[23] The arbitrage benefits result from (a) the exploitation of various institutional imperfections; (b) timing options; (c) technology options; and (d) staging options.[24,25] Better financing bargains[26] as well as capital availability are also possible through internationalization. In addition, multinational firms can achieve arbitrage benefits in financing cash flows by (a) exploiting financial bargains; (b) reducing taxes on financial flows; and (c) mitigating risks or shifting them to agents with a comparative advantage in bearing them.[27] The definition of multinationality as a collection of options and arbitrage benefits suggests a positive relation with growth options as defined by the investment opportunity set. More growth options are more likely to result from increased internationalization. Accordingly, the following hypothesis applies:

H2: Growth opportunities, as measured by the investment opportunity set, vary directly with the level of multinationality.

Size Advantages

Large and more established firms often have advantages over their smaller peers in their ability to exploit emerging opportunities.[28] There is evidence that persistently profitable firms are those that hold the dominant market position in their industry.[29] In addition, large firms are more apt to increase the value of investment options by making differential investments in the creation of barriers to entry that halt or delay the competitive factors that drive returns on investment projects toward the firm's opportunity cost. The generation of economies of scale, product differentiation, brand loyalty, and patents are some examples of these activities.[30] Accordingly, the following hypothesis applies:

H3: Growth opportunities, as measured by the investment opportunity set, vary directly with the size of the firm.

Profitability Advantages

Two seminal papers from financial economics combine to provide a theoretical framework for describing the investment opportunity set. Myers[31] depicts firm value as a combination of income generating assetsin-place (*Va*) and growth opportunities (*Vg*).

$$V = Va + Vg$$

Firms with more assets-in-place have less of their determined growth opportunities and vice versa.

Myers' concept of firm value is consistent with that of Miller and Modigliania[32] (MM), who modeled the value of firm based upon (1) the market rate of return, (2) the earnings power of assets-in-place, and (3) the opportunities for making additional investments in real assets that will yield more than the normal rate of return (i.e., growth opportunities). MM's equation (12) (using their notation) shows the value of the firm (*V*) at time 0:

$$V(0) = \frac{X\,(0)}{\rho} + \sum_{t=0}^{\infty} I(t) \times \frac{\rho^*(t) - \rho}{\rho}\, (1 + \rho)^{-(t+1)}$$

where $X\,(0)$ are earnings from assets-in-place, ρ is the cost of capital, ρ^* is some internal rate of return that exceeds ρ, and I is investment made at time t. The second right-hand-section term encompasses Myers' growth term (*Vg*) and is what is commonly called the investment opportunity set (IOS). Holding firm value constant, the two right-handsection terms are inversely related. This is the "normal" view of growth firms, forgoing earnings from assets-in-place [$X\,(0)$] in the first term, by plowing them back into investment (*I*) in the second term. A recent example is the wireless communication industry the 1980s, showing consistently depressed earnings (and losses) due to significant investments, which combined to result in rapidly increasing firm value.[33] Since both the first and second right-hand-section terms should be correlated with firm value, they are correlated with each other. Accordingly the following hypothesis applies:

H4: Growth opportunities, as measured by the investment opportunity set, vary directly with the level of profitability.

Leverage Limitations

Myers[34] argued that for firms with growth opportunities, the existence of risky debt, maturing after the investment option, causes the firm to forgo profitable investment resulting in an underinvestment scenario. Growth firms tend to issue less debt than firms without growth opportunities because equity financing controls the potential underinvestment problem associated with risky debt.[35] Prior empirical research in financial economics examining the cross-sectional differences in major corporate policy decisions relied on contracting cost explanations and presented empirical evidence regarding the relationship between growth opportunities and leverage.[36,37] Accordingly, the following hypothesis applies:

H5: Growth opportunities, as measured by the investment opportunity set, are negatively related to the level of leverage.

Systematic Risk Limitations

The relationship of the firm's growth opportunities with systematic risk depends on the definition of growth. The definition of growth as expansion yielded a negative relationship between growth and systematic risk.[38-41] The definition of growth as monopoly power in factor and/or output market resulting in larger economic rents also yielded a negative relationship between growth and systematic risk. Finally, the definition of growth as real options yielded a positive relationship between growth and systematic risk.[42,43] On the other hand, Booth[44] and Conine[45] argued that the relationship between growth and beta could be either positive or negative, depending on relative values of other parameters in the model. Accordingly, the following hypothesis applies:

H6: Growth opportunities, as measured by the investment opportunity set, are negatively related to the level of systematic risk.

RESEARCH MODEL

Model

In this study, a regression of the investment opportunity set level of
U.S. MNEs against variables of reputation, multinationality, size, profitability, leverage, and systematic risk is presented as evidence of the
validity of a statement of growth opportunities as follows:

$$IOS_{jt} = \alpha_{0t} + \alpha_{1t}REP_{jt} + \alpha_{2t}MULTY_{jt} + \alpha_{3t}LEV_{jt} + \alpha_{4t}BETA_{jt}$$
$$+ \alpha_{5t}LSIZE_{jt} + \alpha_{6t}ROA_{jt}$$

where:

IOS_{jt} = Investment opportunity set for firm j in year t

REP_{jt} = Corporate reputation for firm j in year t

$MULTY_{jt}$ = Level of multinationality for firm j in year t

LEV_{jt} = Leverage ratio equal to long-term debt/total assets for firm j
in year t

$BETA_{jt}$ = Systematic risk for firm j in year t

$LSIZE_{jt}$ = Logarithm of total assets for firm j in year t

ROA_{jt} = Profitability measured as rate of return on assets of firm j in
year t

Data and Sample Selection

The population consists of firms included in *Forbes'* Most International 100 American manufacturing and service firms and *Fortune's* surveys of corporate reputation from 1987 to 1993. The security data are
collected from the CRSP Return files. The accounting variables are collected from COMPUSTAT. The derivations of multinationality, corporate reputation, systematic risk, and investment opportunity set variables
are explained later. The final sample includes 323 firm-year observations
that have all the variables over the period of analysis.

Measuring Multinationality

Previous research has attempted to measure the following attributes of multinationality:

1. *Performance*—in terms of what goes on overseas[46]
2. *Structure*—in terms of resources used overseas[47]
3. *Attitude or Conduct*—in terms of what is top management's orientation[48]

Sullivan[49] developed nine measures of which five were shown to have a high reliability in the construction of a homogeneous measure of nationality: (1) foreign sales as a percentage of total sales (FSTS), (2) foreign assets over total assets (FATA), (3) overseas subsidiaries as a percentage of total subsidiaries (OSTS), (4) top management's international experience (TMIE), and (5) psychic dispersion of international operations (PDIO).

In this study we follow a similar approach by measuring multinationality through three measures: (1) foreign sales/total sales (FSTS), (2) foreign profits/total profits (FPTP), and (3) foreign assets/total assets (FATA).

Descriptive statistics and correlations among the three multinationality measures are shown in Exhibit 11.2. Correlations among the variables are positive, and with one exception, all significant. The nonsignificant correlation is between FPTP and FATA. The low correlations between FPTP, FSTS, and FATA indicate that each variable can make a unique contribution as a multinationality measure. Thus, a factor analysis of all observations is used to isolate the factor common to the three measures. Exhibit 11.3 reports the results. One common factor appears in the intercorrelations among the three variables, as the first eigenvalue value alone exceeds the sum of the commonalities. The common factor is significantly positively correlated with the three measures. These factor scores were used to measure the degree of multinationality of firms in the sample.

Measuring Corporate Reputation

The *Fortune* survey covers every industry group comprising four or more companies. The industry groups are based on categories established

Exhibit 11.2
Descriptive Statistics and Correlations of Three Measures of
Multinationality for *Forbes'* The Most International 100 U.S. Firms

Panel A: Descriptive Statistics

	FP/TP[a]	FS/TS[b]	FA/TA[c]
Maximum	914.3	93	91
Third Quartile	61.9	47.4	41.4
Median	41.3	36.7	30.5
First Quartile	25	25.7	22.6
Minimum	0.2	6.6	2.7
Mean	52.81	37.45	39.92

Panel B: Correlations

	FP/TP	FS/TS	FA/TA
FP/TP	1.000		
FS/TS	0.280	1.000	
FA/TA	0.034	0.193*	1.000

[a]FP/TP = Foreign profits/total profits
[b]FS/TS = Foreign sales/total sales
[c]FA/TA = Foreign assets/total assets
*Denotes p-value < 0.05.

by the U.S. Office of Management and Budget (OMB). The survey asked executives, directors, and analysts in particular to rate a company on the following eight key attributes of reputation:

1. Quality of management
2. Quality of products/services offered
3. Innovativeness
4. Value as long-term investment
5. Soundness of financial position
6. Ability to attract/develop/keep talented people
7. Responsibility to the community/environment
8. Wise use of corporate assets.

Exhibit 11.3
Selected Statistics Related to a Common Factor Analysis of Three
Measures of Multinationality for *Forbes'* The Most International
100 U.S. Firms

1. Eigenvalues of the Correlation Matrix:

Eigenvalues	1	2	3
	1.3615	0.9680	0.6705

2. Factor Pattern

    FACTOR1

FS/TS	FP/TP	FA/TA
0.80529	0.50172	0.67918
	FA/TA	

3. Final Communality Estimates: Total = 1.361489

FS/TS	FP/TP	FA/TA
0.648491	0.251718	0.461280

4. Standardized Scoring Coefficients

    FACTOR2

FS/TS	FP/TP	FA/TA
0.59148	0.36850	0.49885

5. Descriptive Statistics of the Common Factor Extracted from the Three Measures of

    Multinationality

Maximum	2039.24
Third Quartile	74.70
Median	57.03
First Quartile	40.76
Minimum	5.17
Mean	64.35

Ratings were on a scale of 0 (poor) to 10 (excellent). The score met the multiple-consistency ecological model view of organizational effectiveness. For purposes of our study, the 1987 to 1993 *Fortune* magazine surveys were used. To obtain a unique configuration, a factor analysis is used to isolate the factor common to the eight measures of reputation. All the observations were subjected to factor analysis and one common factor was found to explain the intercorrelations among the eight individual measures. Exhibit 11.4 reports the results of the common factor analysis. One common factor appears to explain the intercorrelations among the eight variables, as the first eigenvalue alone exceeds the sum of the commonalities. The common factor is significantly and positively correlated with the eight measures. The factor scores are used to measure the corporate reputation of firms.

Measuring the Investment Opportunity Set

Because the investment opportunity set is not observable there has not been a consensus on an appropriate proxy variable. Similar to Smith and Watts[50] and Gaver and Gaver[51] we use an ensemble of variables to measure the investment opportunity set. The three measures of the investment opportunity set used are: market to book assets (MASS), market to book equity (MQV), and the earnings/price ratio (EP). These variables are defined as follows:

MASS = [Assets − Total Common Equity + Shares Outstanding* Share
         Closing Price]/Assets
 MQV = [Shares Outstanding* Share Closing Price]/Total Common Eq-
         uity
    EP = [Primary EPS before Extraordinary Items]/Share Closing Price

Descriptive statistics and correlations among the three measures of the investment opportunity set are shown in Exhibit 11.5. Correlations among the three variables are significant. The low correlations indicate that each variable makes a unique contribution as a measure of the investment opportunity set. The results of the factor analysis are shown in Exhibit 11.6. One common factor appears to explain the intercorrelations among the three individual measures. It is used here as a measure of the investment opportunity set.

Exhibit 11.4
Selected Statistics Related to a Common Factor Analysis of Measures of Reputation

1. Eigenvalues of the Correlation Matrix:

   Eigenvalues

1	2	3	4	5	6	$\acute{7}$	8
6.7776	1.4596	0.3841	0.1347	0.1120	0.0549	0.0482	0.0339

2. Factor Pattern

   FACTOR1

R_1	0.9530	R_4	0.9645	R_7	0.8072
R_2	0.9180	R_5	0.8982	R_8	0.9479
R_3	0.8789	R_6	0.9805		

3. Final Communality Estimates: Total = 1.389626

R_1	R_2	R_3	R_4	R_5	R_6	R_7	R_8
0.9083	0.8428	0.7726	0.9304	0.8069	0.9614	0.6515	0.8986

4. Standardized Scoring Coefficients

   FACTOR1

R_1	0.1407	R_4	0.1424	R_7	0.1191
R_2	0.1355	R_5	0.1325	R_8	0.1399
R_3	0.1297	R_6	0.1447		

5. Descriptive Statistics of the Common Factor Extracted from the Three Measures of Multinationality

Third Quartile	7.288
Median	6.614
First Quartile	6.105
Minimum	3.235
Mean	6.622

Variable Definitions
R_1 = Quality of management
R_2 = Quality of products/services
R_3 = Innovativeness
R_4 = Value as long-term investment
R_5 = Soundness of financial position
R_6 = Ability to attract, develop, and keep talented people
R_7 = Responsibility to the community and environment
R_8 = Wise use of corporate assets

Exhibit 11.5
Descriptive Statistics and Correlations of Three Measures of the
Investment Opportunity Set for *Forbes'* The Most International 100 U.S.
Firms

Panel A: Descriptive Statistics

	MASS[a]	MQV[b]	EP[c]
Maximum	6.4943	60	0.5175
Third Quartile	1.8556	3.1851	0.1081
Median	1.2905	1.9090	0.0713
First Quartile	1.0618	1.2666	0.0482
Minimum	0.8745	4.3333	2.1536
Mean	0.3081	2.7020	0.0638

Panel B: Correlation

	MASS	MQV	EP
MASS	1.000		
MQV	0.0399*	1.000	
EP	0.0158*	0.0230*	1.000

[a]MASS = Market-to-book assets
[b]MQV = Market-to-book equity
[c]EP   = Earnings/price ratio
*Denotes *p*-value < 0.05.

Measuring the Systematic Risk

The capital asset pricing model asserts that in equilibrium, and under certain conditions, the risk premium for an individual security, $E(\tilde{R}_i)$ − $E(\tilde{R}_F)$ is related to the risk premium of the market, $E(\tilde{R}_m)$ − $E(\tilde{R}_F)$ by the expression

$$E(\tilde{R}_i) - E(\tilde{R}_F) = [E(\tilde{R}_m) - E(\tilde{R}_F)]\beta i$$

where:

$E(\tilde{R}_F)$ = risk-free rate

$E(\tilde{R}_m)$ = expected return on a market factor

$\beta i = \text{cov}(\tilde{R}_i, \tilde{R}_m)/\text{var}(\tilde{R}_m)$

βi is a measure of the systematic of nondiversifiable risk. Its estimation is operationally possible using the one-factor market model, which asserts a linear relationship between the rate of return on security i, R_{it}, and the market rate of return, R_{mt}, for a period t. It is expressed in this study as follows:

$$r_{it} = \alpha I + \beta r_{mt} + e_{it}$$
$$E\{e_{it}\} = O$$
$$E\{e^2_{it}\} = N^0$$
$$E\{e_{it} \cdot e_{ik}\} = O, \forall\, k \neq t$$
$$E\{e_{st} \cdot e_{it}\} = O, \forall\, s \neq I$$
$$E\{\ln\{r^2_m\} \cdot e_{it}\} = O$$

where:

r_{it} = continuously compounded rate of return of security i at period t

$\quad = \log_e(I + R_{it})$

$\quad = \log_e[(P_t + D_t)/P_{t-1}]$

R_{it} = noncompounded single-period return of security i in period t

r_m = market factor in period t $\log_e$

e_{it} = logarithm of the residual term

D_{it} = cash dividend per share

α_I, β_i = parameters of the least-squares regression

r_{it} is used instead of R_{it} because it is admitted that, first, r_{it} has fewer outliers in its relative frequency distribution and therefore will yield more efficient risk statistics than R_{it}, and second, r_{it} is distributed more symmetrically than the positively skewed R_{it} variable. Besides, the results of

Exhibit 11.6

Selected Statistics Related to a Common Factor Analysis of Three Measures of the Investment Opportunity Set for *Forbes'* The Most International 100 U.S. Firms

1. Eigenvalues of the Correlation Matrix: Total = 3 Average = 1

Eigenvalues	1	2	3
	1.0540	0.9868	0.9592

2. Factor Pattern

   FACTOR1

	MASS	MQV	EP
	0.62821	0.66411	0.46722

3. Final Communality Estimates: Total = 1.053994

	MASS	MQV	EP
	0.394651	0.441045	0.218299

4. Standardized Scoring Coefficients

   FACTOR1

	MASS	MQV	EP
	0.59603	0.441045	0.44329

5. Descriptive Statistics of the Common Factor Extracted from the Three Measures of the Investment

   Opportunity

Maximum	9.3595
Third Quartile	3.2200
Median	2.0450
First Quartile	1.5085
Minimum	2.5209
Means	1.9812

the model are not changed by restating them in terms of r_{it} instead of R_{it}.

RESULTS

Panel A of Exhibit 11.7 reports descriptive statistics used in our tests and panel B shows correlations among the variables. The correlations reported in panel B of Exhibit 11.7 show that some correlations are significant at the 0.01 level. The significant associations among some of the variables indicate some degree of collinearity among the independent variables in the regression analysis. However, the maximum-condition index in all regression is only 4.43. As suggested by Belsley et al.[52] mild collinearity is diagnosed for maximum-condition indices between 5 and 10 and severe collinearity over 30. Thus, collinearity does not seem to influence our results.

For the multivariate regression to be reported, we performed additional specification tests, including checks for normality and consideration of a scatter plot. A null hypothesis of normality could not be rejected at the 0.01 level in all cases, and the plots revealed some heteroscedasticity but no obvious problems. Therefore, we calculated the t-statistics after correcting for heteroscedasticity in the manner described by White.[53]

Exhibit 11.8 presents the results of the regression of the determinants of the investment opportunity set. The regression was significant with an F-value of 23.798. The independent variables explained 30.28 percent of the variance in the dependent variable of the investment opportunity set. As expected, all the independent variables were significant with the correct sign. Growth opportunities, as measured by the investment opportunity set, are positively related to the level of corporate reputation, multinationality, size, and profitability and negatively related to leverage and systematic risk. The results verified the statement of a general model of growth opportunities.

CONCLUSIONS

A general model of growth opportunities combining the advantages of corporate reputation, multinationality, size, and profitability and the limitations of leverage and systematic risk is tested using a sample of U.S. MNEs. The evidence validates this statement of growth opportunities by showing that growth opportunities, as measured by the investment opportunity set, are positively related to corporate reputation,

Exhibit 11.7
Descriptive Statistics and Correlations

Panel A: Descriptive Statistics

Variable	Mean	Standard Deviation	Maximum	Median	Minimum
IOS	18.552	15.073	117.006	1.930	0.695
MULTY	54.324	28.357	325.478	51.274	6.210
LEV	0.354	0.187	1.44	0.374	0.257
BETA	0.009	0.013	1.104	0.004	0.021
LSIZE	9.325	1.106	12.353	9.073	7.617
ROA	0.057	0.056	0.221	0.057	0.021
REP	6.622	0.968	9.022	6.614	3.235

Panel B: Correlations

Variables	IOS	REP	MULTY	LEV	BETA	LSIZE	ROA
IOS	1.000						
REP	0.1804	1.000					
MULTY	0.0834	-0.0504	1.000				
LEV	-0.4205[a]	0.3054[a]	0.0850[b]	1.000			
BETA	-0.0695	0.4574[a]	0.0634	0.1781[a]	1.000		
LSIZE	0.3719	0.0150	-0.0554	-0.3972[a]	0.4557[a]	1.000	
ROA	-0.2546[b]	0.5352[a]	-0.1123[a]	0.4597[a]	0.2230[a]	-0.2996[a]	

[a]Significant at the 0.01 level.
[b]Significant at the 0.05 level.
Variable Definitions
IOS   = Investment opportunity set
REP   = Reputation score
MULTY = Multinationality score
LEV   = Leverage ratio
LSIZE   = Logarithm of total assets
BETA   = Systematic risk
ROA   = Rate of return on assets

Exhibit 11.8
Regression Results

Variables	Coefficient
Intercept	-.387.533 (-5.604)[a]
REP	17.200 (3.215)[a]
MULTY	0.682 (3.619)[a]
LEV	-137.029 (-4.552)[a]
BETA	-2098.43 (-5.214)[a]
LSIZE	33.564 (5.453)[a]
ROA	185.340 (3.451)[a]
F	23.798 [a]
Adjusted R²	30.28%

[a]Significant at the 0.01 level.
Variable Definitions
REP   = Reputation score
MULTY = Multinationality score
LEV   = Leverage ratio
BETA   = Systematic risk
LSIZE = Logarithm of total assets
ROA   = Rate of return on assets

multinationality, size, and profitability and negatively related to leverage and systematic risk. The results are dependent on the choice of surrogate measures for both dependent and independent variables. Future research needs to examine the sensitivity of the results to other potential surrogate measures.

NOTES

1. S. Myers, "Determinants of Corporate Borrowing," *Journal of Financial Economics* 5 (1977): 147–175.

2. W. C. Kester, "Today's Options for Tomorrow's Growth," *Harvard Business Review* (March-April 1984): 153–160.

3. S. P. Mason and R. C. Merton, "The Role of Contingent Claims Analysis in Corporate Finance." In E. I. Altman, ed., *Recent Advances in Corporate Finance* (Homewood, IL: Irwin, 1985): 7–54.

4. Kester, "Today's Options for Tomorrow's Growth," 153–160.

5. W. C. Kester, "An Option Approach to Corporate Finance," ch. 5. In E. I. Altman, ed., *Handbook of Corporate Finance* (New York: Wiley, 1986): 3–35.

6. R. Pimdyck, "Irreversible Investment, Capacity Choice, and the Value of the Firm," *American Economic Review* (December 1988): 969–985.

7. C. Smith and R. Watts, "The Investment Opportunity Set and Corporate Financing, Dividend, and Compensation Policies," *Journal of Financial Economics* 32 (1992): 263–292.

8. Baber, W. R., S. N. Janakiraman, and Kang Sok-Hyon, "Investment Opportunities and the Structure of Executive Compensation," *Journal of Accounting and Economics* 21 (1996): 297–318.

9. D. J. Skinner, "The Investment Opportunity Set and Accounting Procedure Choice," *Journal of Accounting and Economics* 16 (1993): 403–445.

10. J. A. Miles, "Growth Options and the Real Determinants of Systematic Risk," *Journal of Business Finance and Accounting* 13 (1986): 95–105.

11. J. J. Gaver and K. M. Gaver, "Additional Evidence on the Association between the Investment Opportunity Set and Corporate Financing, Dividend and Compensation Policies," *Journal of Accounting and Economics* 16 (1993): 125–160.

12. A. Riahi-Belkaoui and R. D. Picur, "Multinationality and Profitability: The Contingency of the Investment Opportunity Set," *Managerial Finance* (1998).

13. G. R. Dowling, "Managing Your Corporate Images," *Industrial Marketing Management* 15 (1986): 109–115.

14. A. Riahi-Belkaoui and E. Pavlik, *Accounting for Corporate Reputation* (Westport, CT: Greenwood Publishing, 1992). A. Riahi-Belkaoui and E. Pavlik,

"Asset Management Performance and Reputation Building for Large U.S. Firms," *British Journal of Management* 2 (1191): 231–238.

15. A. M. Spencer, *Market Signaling: Information Transfer in Hiring and Related Screening Process* (Cambridge, MA: Harvard University Press, 1974).

16. C. Fombrum and M. Shanley, "What's in a Name? Reputational Building and Corporate Strategy," *Academy of Management Journal* 33 (1990): 233–258.

17. A. Belakoui, "Organizational Effectiveness, Social Performance and Economic Performance," *Research in Corporate Social Performance and Policy* 12 (1992): 143–155.

18. Riahi-Belkaoui and Pavlik, "Asset Management Performance and Reputation Building for Large U.S. Firms," 231–238.

19. Fombrum and Shanley, "What's in a Name? Reputational Building and Corporate Strategy," 233–258.

20. R. E. Caves and M. E. Porter, "From Entry Barrier to Mobility Barriers," *Quarterly Journal of Economics* 91 (1977): 421–434.

21. B. Klein and K. Leffler, "The Role of Market Forces in Assuring Contractual Performance," *Journal of Political Economy* 85 (1981): 615–641.

22. R. P. Beatty and J. R. Ritter, "Investment Banking, Reputation, and Underpricing of Initial Public Offerings," *Journal of Financial Economics* 15 (1986): 213–232.

23. G. P. Tsetsekos, "Multinationality and Common Stock Offering," *Journal of International Business Studies* 25 (1991): 325–342.

24. J. H. Dunning, "Reappraising the Eclectic Paradigm in an Age of Alliance Capitalism," *Journal of International Business Studies* 26 (1995), 461–492.

25. B. Kogut, "Foreign Direct Investment as a Sequential Process." In C. P. Kindelberger and D. B. Audretsch, eds., *The Multinational Corporation in the 1980s* (Cambridge, MA: MIT Press, 1983): 38–56.

26. F. Giavazzi and A. Giovannini, *Limiting Exchange Rate Flexibility: The European Monetary System.* (Cambridge, MA: MIT Press, 1989).

27. Tsetsekos, "Multinationality and Common Stock Offering," 325–342.

28. Gaver and Gaver, "Additional Evidence on the Association between the Investment Opportunity Set and Corporate Financing, Dividend and Compensation Policies," 125–160.

29. D. Mueller, "Persistent Performance among Large Corporations." In L. G. Thomas III, ed., *The Economics of Strategic Planning: Essays in Honor of Joel Dean* (Lexington, MA: D. C. Heath, 1986): 31–61.

30. K. H. Chung and C. Charroenwong, "Investment Options, Assets in Place, and the Risk of Stocks," *Financial Management* (Autumn 1991): 21–33.

31. Myers, "Determinants of Corporate Borrowing," 147–175.

32. M. H. Miller and F. Modigliani, "Dividend Policy, Growth, and the Valuation of Shares," *Journal of Business* 4 (1961): 411–433.

33. Eli Amir and B. Lev, "Value-Relevance of Nonfinancial Information: The Wireless Communications Industry," *Journal of Accounting and Economics* 22 (1996): 3–30.

34. Myers, "Determinants of Corporate Borrowing," 147–175.

35. Ibid.

36. Gaver and Gaver, "Additional Evidence on the Association between the Investment Opportunity Set and Corporate Financing, Dividend and Compensation Policies," 125–160.

37. Smith and Watts, "The Investment Opportunity Set and Corporate Financing, Dividend, and Compensation Policies," 263–292.

38. W. Beaver, P. Kettler, and M. Scholes, "The Association between Market-Determined and Accounting-Determined Risk Measures," *Accounting Review* (October 1970): 654–682.

39. R. Pettit and R. Westerfield, "A Model of Capital Asset Risk," *Journal of Financial and Quantitative Analysis* (March 1972): 1649–1688.

40. W. Breen and E. Lerner, "Corporate Financial Strategies and Market Measures of Risk and Return," *Journal of Finance* (May 1973): 339–352.

41. D. Thompson, "Sources of Systematic Risk to Common Stocks," *Journal of Business* (April 1976): 173–188.

42. R. Eskew, "The Forecasting Ability of Accounting Risk Measures: Some Additional Evidence," *Accounting Review* (January 1979): 107–118.

43. A. Christie, "Equity Risk, the Opportunity Set, Production Costs and Debt," Working paper (Rochester, NY: University of Rochester, 1989). Chung and Charroenwong, "Investment Options, Assets in Place, and the Risk of Stocks," 21–33.

44. L. Booth, "Market Structure Uncertainty and the Cost of Equity Capital," *Journal of Banking and Finance* 3 (1981): 467–482.

45. J. Conine, "On the Theoretical Relationship between Business Risk and Price Elasticity of Demand," *Journal of Business Finance and Accounting* 3 (1983): 173–182.

46. Dunning, "Reappraising the Eclectic Paradigm in an Age of Alliance Capitalism," 461–492.

47. J. M. Stopford and L. T. Wells, *Managing the Multinational Enterprise* (New York: Basic Books, 1972).

48. H. V. Perlmutter, "The Tortuous Evaluation of the Multinational Corporation," *Columbia Journal of World Business* 4 (1969): 9–18.

49. D. Sullivan, "Measuring the Degree of Internationalization of a Firm," *Journal of International Business Studies* 25 (1994): 325–342.

50. Smith and Watts, "The Investment Opportunity Set and Corporate Financing, Dividend, and Compensation Policies," 263–292.

51. Gaver and Gaver, "Additional Evidence on the Association between the Investment Opportunity Set and Corporate Financing, Dividend and Compensation Policies," 125–160.

52. D. Belsley, E. Kuh, and R. Welsch, *Regression Diagnostics: Identifying Influential Data and Sources of Collinearity* (New York: Wiley, 1980).

53. H. A. White, "Heteroskedasticity-Consistent Covariance Matrix Estimator and a Direct Test for Heteroskedasticity," *Econometrika* 10 (1980): 817–838.

SELECTED READINGS

Amir, Eli, and B. Lev. "Value-Relevance of Nonfinancial Information: The Wireless Communications Industry." *Journal of Accounting and Economics* 22 (1996): 3–30.

Baber, W. R., S. N. Janakiraman, and Kang Sok-Hyon. "Investment Opportunities and the Structure of Executive Compensation." *Journal of Accounting and Economics* 21 (1996): 297–318.

Beatty, R. P., and J. R. Ritter. "Investment Banking, Reputation, and Underpricing of Initial Public Offerings." *Journal of Financial Economics* 15 (1986): 213–232.

Beaver, W., P. Kettler, and M. Scholes. "The Association between Market-Determined and Accounting-Determined Risk Measures." *Accounting Review* (October 1970): 654–682.

Belkaoui, A. "Organizational Effectiveness, Social Performance and Economic Performance." *Research in Corporate Social Performance and Policy* 12 (1992): 143–155.

Belsley, D., E. Kuh, and R. Welsch. *Regression Diagnostics: Identifying Influential Data and Sources of Collinearity*. New York: Wiley, 1980.

Booth, L. "Market Structure Uncertainty and the Cost of Equity Capital." *Journal of Banking and Finance* 3 (1981): 467–482.

Breen, W., and E. Lerner. "Corporate Financial Strategies and Market Measures of Risk and Return." *Journal of Finance* (May 1973): 339–352.

Caves, R. E., and M. E. Porter. "From Entry Barrier to Mobility Barriers." *Quarterly Journal of Economics* 91 (1977): 421–434.

Christie, A. "Equity Risk, the Opportunity Set, Production Costs and Debt." Working paper. Rochester, NY: University of Rochester, 1989.

Chung, K. H., and C. Charroenwong. "Investment Options, Assets in Place, and the Risk of Stocks." *Financial Management* (Autumn 1991): 21–33.

Conine, J. "On the Theoretical Relationship between Business Risk and Price Elasticity of Demand." *Journal of Business Finance and Accounting* 3 (1983): 173–182.

Dowling, G. R. "Managing Your Corporate Images." *Industrial Marketing Management* 15 (1986): 109–115.

Dunning, J. H. "Reappraising the Eclectic Paradigm in an Age of Alliance Capitalism." *Journal of International Business Studies* 26 (1995): 461–492.

Eskew, R. "The Forecasting Ability of Accounting Risk Measures: Some Additional Evidence," *Accounting Review* (January 1979): 107–118.

Fombrum, C., and M. Shanley. "What's in a Name? Reputational Building and Corporate Strategy." *Academy of Management Journal* 33 (1990): 233–258.

Gaver, J. J., and K. M. Gaver. "Additional Evidence on the Association between the Investment Opportunity Set and Corporate Financing, Dividend and Compensation Policies." *Journal of Accounting and Economics* 16 (1993): 125–160.

Giavazzi, F., and A. Giovannini. *Limiting Exchange Rate Flexibility: The European Monetary* System. Cambridge, MA: MIT Press, 1989.

Kester, W. C. "Today's Options for Tomorrow's Growth." *Harvard Business Review* (March-April 1984): 153–160.

———. "An Option Approach to Corporate Finance," ch. 5. In E. I. Altman, ed. *Handbook of Corporate Finance.* New York: Wiley, 1986: 3–35.

Klein, B., and K. Leffler. "The Role of Market Forces in Assuring Contractual Performance." *Journal of Political Economy* 85 (1981): 615–641.

Kogut, B. "Foreign Direct Investment as a Sequential Process." In C. Kindelberger and D. Audretsch, eds., *The Multinational Corporation in the 1980s.* Cambridge, MA: MIT Press, 1983: 38–56.

Mason, S. P., and R. C. Merton. "The Role of Contingent Claims Analysis in Corporate Finance." In E. I. Altman, ed. *Recent Advances in Corporate Finance.* Homewood, IL: Irwin, 1985: 7–54.

Miles, J. A. "Growth Options and the Real Determinants of Systematic Risk." *Journal of Business Finance and Accounting* 13 (1986): 95–105.

Miller, M. H., and F. Modigliani. "Dividend Policy, Growth, and the Valuation of Shares." *Journal of Business* 4 (1961): 411–433.

Mueller, D. "Persistent Performance among Large Corporations." In L. G. Thomas III, ed. *The Economics of Strategic Planning: Essays in Honor of Joel Dean.* Lexington, MA: D. C. Heath, 1986: 31–61.

Myers, S. "Determinants of Corporate Borrowing." *Journal of Financial Economics* 5 (1977): 147–175.

Perlmutter, H. V. "The Tortuous Evaluation of the Multinational Corporation." *Columbia Journal of World Business* 4 (1969): 9–18.

Pettit, R., and R. Westerfield. "A Model of Capital Asset Risk." *Journal of Financial and Quantitative Analysis* (March 1972): 1649–1688.

Pimdyck, R. "Irreversible Investment, Capacity Choice, and the Value of the Firm." *American Economic Review* (December 1988): 969–985.

Riahi-Belkaoui, A. *International and Multinational Accounting.* International Thomson Business Press, 1994.

Riahi-Belkaoui, A., and E. Pavlik. "Asset Management Performance and Reputation Building for Large U.S. Firms." *British Journal of Management* 2 (1991): 231–238.

————. *Accounting for Corporate Reputation.* Westport, CT: Greenwood Publishing, 1992.

Riahi-Belkaoui, A., and R. D. Picur. "Multinationality and Profitability: The Contingency of the Investment Opportunity Set." *Managerial Finance* (1998).

Rosenberg, B., and W. McKibben. "The Prediction of Systematic and Specific Risk in Common Stock." *Journal of Financial and Quantitative Analysis* (March 1973): 317–334.

Skinner, D. J. "The Investment Opportunity Set and Accounting Procedure Choice." *Journal of Accounting and Economics* 16 (1993): 403–445.

Smith, C., and R. Watts. "The Investment Opportunity Set and Corporate Financing, Dividend, and Compensation Policies." *Journal of Financial Economics* 32 (1992): 263–292.

Spencer, A. M. *Market Signaling: Information Transfer in Hiring and Related Screening Process.* Cambridge, MA: Harvard University Press, 1974.

Stopford, J. M., and L. T. Wells. *Managing the Multinational Enterprise.* New York: Basic Books, 1972.

Sullivan, D. "Measuring the Degree of Internationalization of a Firm." *Journal of International Business Studies* 25 (1994): 325–342.

Thompson, D. "Sources of Systematic Risk to Common Stocks." *Journal of Business* (April 1976): 173–188.

Tsetsekos, G. P. "Multinationality and Common Stock Offering." *Journal of International Business Studies* 25 (1991): 325–342.

White, H. A. "Heteroskedasticity-Consistent Covariance Matrix Estimator and a Direct Test for Heteroskedasticity." *Econometrika* 10 (1980): 817–838.

Index

About the Author

AHMED RIAHI-BELKAOUI is CBA Distinguished Professor of Accounting in the College of Business Administration, University of Illinois at Chicago. Author of more than 30 Quorum books and coauthor of several more, he is also a prolific author of articles published in major scholarly and professional journals, and has served on numerous editorial boards.

ISBN 1-56720-277-2

EAN

9 781567 202779

90000>

HARDCOVER BAR CODE